Better Homes and Gardens®

WORKING AT HOME

BETTER HOMES AND GARDENS® BOOKS

Editor: Gerald M. Knox
Art Director: Ernest Shelton
Managing Editor: David A. Kirchner
Copy and Production Editors: Marsha Jahns,
Mary Helen Schiltz, Carl Voss, David A. Walsh

Associate Art Directors: Linda Ford Vermie, Neoma Alt West,
Randall Yontz
Assistant Art Directors: Faith Berven, Harijs Priekulis,
Tom Wegner
Senior Graphic Designers: Alisann Dixon, Lynda Haupert,
Lyne Neymeyer
Graphic Designers: Mike Burns, Mike Eagleton, Deb Miner,
Stan Sams, Darla Whipple

Vice President, Editorial Director: Doris Eby
Group Editorial Services Director: Duane L. Gregg

Senior Vice President, General Manager: Fred Stines
Director of Publishing: Robert B. Nelson
Vice President, Retail Marketing: Jamie Martin
Vice President, Direct Marketing: Arthur Heydendael

All About Your House: Working at Home

Project Editor: James A. Hufnagel
Associate Editors: Leonore A. Levy,
Willa Rosenblatt Speiser
Copy and Production Editor: Marsha Jahns
Building and Remodeling Editor: Joan McCloskey
Furnishings and Design Editor: Shirley Van Zante
Garden Editor: Douglas A. Jimerson
Money Management and Features Editor: Margaret Daly

Associate Art Director: Neoma Alt West
Graphic Designer: Stan Sams
Electronic Text Processor: Donna Russell

Contributing Editors: Stephen Mead and Jill Abeloe Mead
Contributors: Cathy Howard, Jamie Laughridge, Leonore A. Levy,
Willa Rosenblatt Speiser, Carl Voss

Special thanks to Carol Bruns, Stow/Davis, William N. Hopkins,
Bill Hopkins, Jr., Babs Klein, Sue Lewis, Ahern-Pershing Office
Supplies and Equipment Co., Kathy Stechert, and
Don Wipperman for their valuable contributions to this book.

INTRODUCTION

Many of the books in the ALL ABOUT YOUR HOUSE Library focus specifically on individual areas of your home—its kitchen, for example, or bath, or bedrooms; others emphasize wide-ranging improvements you can make, such as furnishing and decorating, even renewing or remodeling, an entire house. Unlike these volumes, *Working at Home* concentrates on an activity: working in your home—to earn a living, to keep the house running smoothly, or to find personal fulfillment. With more than 150 plans, illustrations, and color photographs, *Working at Home* continues the ALL ABOUT YOUR HOUSE blend of practicality and inspiration, but here you'll also meet people who have successfully incorporated businesses and major avocations into their households.

In researching this book, we've discovered that the numbers of at-home workers have increased dramatically over the past decade or so. And if attitude surveys are correct, even more people would like to forgo the 9-to-5 routine so they can integrate their professional and personal lives.

If you're thinking about launching a home-based business, the pages that follow present examples galore—quarters for everyone from architects and artists to weavers and woodworkers. Working at home requires more than just a well-outfitted space, however, so we've included a chapter that guides you through the legal, financial, and tax complexities of being your own boss, and gives you pointers about the all-important process of finding buyers for your goods or services. Of course, making a living at home isn't to everyone's taste, and for many it's simply not possible. But what family couldn't benefit from a well-organized planning center, appealing kids' study spaces, a bedroom desk for briefcase work, or a puttering place for repair and improvement jobs? *Working at Home* includes lots of these types of home work centers, too. As with other volumes in the ALL ABOUT YOUR HOUSE Library, we hope this one will help your house work harder for you.

WORKING
AT HOME

CONTENTS

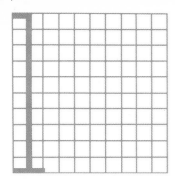

EVALUATING YOUR NEEDS FOR HOME WORK SPACE

Though most of us tend to think of home as a place to relax, there come times when, even at home, we have to roll up our sleeves and get to work. Bill-paying, schoolwork, after-hours paperwork, and hobbies are all integral parts of domestic life. More and more, working at home also is becoming an accepted part of business and professional life. In this chapter we'll help you identify space needs for all kinds of activities. In later chapters, you'll see where the successful search for work space may take you, and then meet a variety of people who've brought the phrase "working at home" to life in their own homes.

HOW CAN YOU SET UP A HOME OFFICE?

Although home work activities vary widely, they all require some type of home office or work center. Because home offices must meet such disparate needs, they come in all sizes, styles, and degrees of formality. How much space you allot to your home office depends on how you plan to use it and how much space you have to work with.

You may not need a lot of space—in fact, you probably need less actual floor space than you might think. If the activity you'd like to carry out in your home requires few specialized accessories, then a desk, a chair, and good lighting are all you need. Setting up the basics attractively and efficiently is the key.

An unused corner of a heavily used room may be appropriate if you don't need a lot of privacy and don't mind listening to household sounds as you work. For more privacy, but still only minimal insulation from routine household noise, consider small, easily overlooked spaces such as the section of a hallway between the last doorway and the end wall. These will put you out of the mainstream of activity without completely shutting you off from it.

Shared space
The colorful design center pictured *opposite* is right at home in a corner of a general-purpose den. The drafting table has a see-through drawing board that rotates 360 degrees and tilts 90 degrees. The stool is designed for people who work standing up. Vital accessories that combine practicality with good looks include a compact telephone, articulated desk lamp, and collapsible storage baskets mounted on a wheeled rack.

Another way to develop office space within a room is by installing a divider. You can partition a living room or family room with a home-built room divider or with purchased screens. The privacy this type of setting will give you may be just the added "official" stamp of serious purpose you need to get started in your home.

Other sources of work space include garages, attics, basements, bedrooms vacated by grown-up children, spare rooms, even closets. To learn more about identifying possible sites for home offices, see Chapter 2—"Where to Find Work Space."

Special space
The *kind* of space you require is an important factor, too. Privacy and quiet may well be top priorities for your home work space, but they may not be the only considerations. Do you need running water, natural light, telephone lines? Is the work center a place where you will meet with other people? Will your visitors be clients, employees, people you already know? What kind of public area, if any, will you need? Does your work space have to deliver a message to the public, or does it just have to work for you? What about parking and seating? Will your activities have any impact on the neighbors? (If so—and sometimes even if not—you should check zoning and other regulations.)

For more information about establishing a home work center and tailoring space to suit your needs, see Chapter 7—"Home Business Basics"; Chapter 8—"At-Home Offices"; and Chapter 9—"Other Home-Based Businesses."

EVALUATING YOUR NEEDS FOR HOME WORK SPACE

HAVE YOU ALWAYS WANTED TO WORK AT HOME?

Avoiding rush hour traffic, not sitting (or standing) on stalled trains or buses, becoming attuned to the seasons and to the daily rhythm of your home and neighborhood life. These are all appealing prospects, and working at home offers them. Some jobs, in certain offices, in factories, and in schools, undeniably demand your physical presence. But, increasingly, there are job options that allow for at least some time to be spent working at home.

Start by asking yourself two key questions. First, do you have a portable product or a service that people will come to you for? Second, what about that intangible factor, discipline—in other words, can you work without direction and encouragement from a nearby co-worker or supervisor? If you say yes to both, working at home may be a more attainable dream than you've realized.

Your work center can be a kitchen if you're a caterer, a den outfitted with a computer if you're a writer or accountant, or the whole house if you're an innkeeper—or homemaker. To learn how more than a dozen people turned their goal of working at home into reality, see chapters 8 and 9—"At-Home Offices" and "Other Home-Based Businesses." For more about home management centers, see Chapter 3.

Although a well-decorated work center can't take the place of good work, surroundings *are* important. Whether you're a home-based professional, craftsperson, or entrepreneur, working at home is a state of mind as much as a change of location. A businesslike setting with just a few special touches can be a big help, not necessarily to impress outsiders, but to reinforce your own attitudes and remind you that you're at work even though you're at home.

The home office pictured *at left* illustrates this. It is set up like many other offices, complete with a laminate-top desk, roll-around chair, and low-maintenance plants. But the purple background wall and matching plush carpet, as well as the louvered wood door and turn-of-the-century hall tree, personalize this home office and set it apart from its away-from-home peers.

IS THERE A HOME COMPUTER IN YOUR FUTURE?

Personal computers do everything from storing recipes and keeping track of household finances to entertaining your children and helping you write books. As an aid in both home management and home-based business, a computer can be a valued new friend. If you don't have one, you probably know families who do. And if you think you will be getting a computer in the foreseeable future, the more you know about what computers can do for you and what they need to keep them working smoothly, the better.

The pine-accented computer room pictured *below* started life as a standard den. It's living proof that any room equipped with electricity has the potential to become a true computer center. The computer sits on a caster-mounted cart that rolls out of the way if the room is needed for other activities. As a result, the room serves as both an up-to-the-minute office and a comfortable family room—the electronic cottage at its homiest.

For a more compact approach, look at the neon-accented room shown *opposite*.

Look again, and you'll discover that this high-tech work center is an electronic closet, in this case a large walk-in closet with the door removed. Built-ins provide storage and counter space. The laminate surface has a matte finish to minimize glare; a rubber floor mat reduces static buildup—an important consideration when you're working with a computer—and makes it easier to roll the desk chair. A slit in the countertop accommodates the printer's paper, which is stored in a lower cabinet.

These computer rooms show only two of the possibili-ties for fitting a computer into your home. For all their versatility and high-tech magic, computers themselves take up about as much space as a typewriter or television set. The more peripherals (auxiliary equipment) you have, however, the more room you'll need.

If you plan to purchase a computer, apply the same principles you would for setting up any work center. See chapters 2 and 4 for general pointers. For more about the special needs of computers and how to coordinate their needs with your own, see pages 40-43.

ARE YOU AN ARTIST?

It may be true that creativity will always find a way to express itself, but lack of space can certainly impede the process—at least for some forms of creative expression. No matter how efficiently you store tools and materials, you'll need generously dimensioned work areas for many pursuits—weaving, sculpting, and painting, for example. Carving out a studio for yourself may not be as hard a job as it seems, however; the key may be as basic as clearing out a garage or as complex as adding a new wing to your home. And if studio space is available, but not as large as you'd like, making the space *look* larger than it really is—mirrors help—and arranging furnishings and equipment to make the best use of the space you have may be more than half the battle.

The skylighted studio pictured *at right* combines two approaches to gaining space: adaptation and adding on. It occupies what was once open-air space above a multicar garage. Thanks to well-planned construction, the studio is easily accessible from the family room, has running water and an adjacent bath, and captures daylight through skylight panels and a wall of fixed glass. Supply cabinets and files line up along a dramatic stone wall.

Not all artistic activities require this combination of features. For a photographer, windows in a darkroom are a disadvantage; for a potter, windows are pleasant but not essential; for a weaver or needlecrafter, running water is a convenience but certainly not a necessity. What kind of space you need depends on the nature of your art. For more about how a variety of home-based artists have found or created space to meet their special needs, see Chapter 5—"Artists' Quarters."

Where you find space, however, has less to do with what you do than with what's available. You may have a garage or shed that can be converted easily to craft space, or an attic that needs only a simple skylight to turn it into a classic studio. Or, you may be able to modify or expand existing space in more limited areas—by bumping-out from the family room, for example, to create a weaver's alcove. A basement corner is fine for a darkroom, and might even do for certain types of design activity, though lighting needs would require careful consideration. For more suggestions about finding or creating work space, see Chapter 2.

HAVE YOUR HOBBIES
TAKEN OVER THE HOUSE?

It's often hard to strike an acceptable balance between home and hobby. Sometimes you get so involved with a hobby that it dominates several rooms, and the dining table or kitchen cabinets lose their identities. At the other end of the scale, you may feel you have no room for your hobby equipment, and keep it so carefully stored out of the way that you rarely get around to enjoying the activity. But somewhere in your home you're likely to find a place you can adapt for hobbies, a place that's convenient but not in the way, where you can spend leisure time on a project that's both worthwhile and recreational.

The craftsman pictured *opposite* put his hobby to work creating hobby space for himself. His shop was once a closet, and he used his tools and skills to convert it to a workshop. His sawing jig, for example, is simply two boards that bridge the width of the closet. The walls are lined with perforated hardboard to provide ample storage space for a well-chosen collection of tools.

The colorful craft center pictured *at left* takes advantage of closet space, too. The shelves are mounted on wood ledgers that are securely attached to the closet walls; hangable objects are stored on perforated hardboard. The secret here, and in many other hobby centers, is to use existing space to best advantage. Make full use of the storage capacity of walls, and choose equipment carefully. Don't purchase more tools than you can really use and store conveniently. Be creative when it comes to putting things away; adapt everyday items such as plastic bins, wicker baskets, and lumber, wherever you can.

You may not have extra closet space—or you may have a whole basement, attic, or garage that could be converted to hobby space. Whether your main concern is finding a nook or cranny, or the very different "problem" of turning unused space into used space, see pages 28 and 29 for space-maximizing ideas. For more about workshops, see Chapter 6. Even if your hobby is not one of those discussed, you'll find plenty of ideas that you can apply to your own home. And for a potpourri of hobby centers and solutions to space and storage needs, see Chapter 10— "A Place for Your Hobby."

DO YOU NEED A FULL-SCALE WORKSHOP?

Few activities are as satisfying as making something that looks good, works well, or tastes delicious. The satisfaction doesn't come from making money—although that may well be an added benefit—but from knowing you've used your talent to produce something worthwhile. Whether you need space to spread out your materials, good lighting so you can see what you're doing, or a soundproof area where your tools won't be a noise nuisance to others, finding the right place can be a challenge. Here are points to consider when you're seeking a site for a shop.

The folk artist pictured here practices an updated version of a traditional craft. He makes weather vanes (the traditional part) with brightly painted decorative figures out of sheet metal and wood (the updated part). And, as you can see, it is a craft that takes up lots of room. Among his needs: good lighting, and storage space for materials and projects. There's one unusual requirement, too: open-air space where new sheet metal can weather. The answer for this folk artist and his wife (her quilting studio is shown on pages 76 and 77) was a new building constructed on the foundation of an old barn.

The ground level includes storage for materials and equipment too unwieldy for this upper-level shop. Plenty of windows and several skylights (not shown) bring in light; industrial-style incandescent fixtures illuminate the work area at night. A door in the background of the photo *at right* leads downstairs and outside.

If your shop needs are less complex than this, you could consider expanding a basement workroom, or planning an arrangement that lets your car and your craft share the garage. To learn about the basics of setting up a variety of shops—from a simple bench for puttering to a full-scale furniture-maker's facility—see pages 82-97. Realize, too, that zoning and use ordinances could preclude your setting up a professional workshop. To learn about these, turn to pages 102 and 103.

DO YOUR CHILDREN HAVE THEIR OWN PLACES TO WORK?

Children lead busy lives, and many of their activities constitute work in some sense—homework, cleanup tasks, even learning basic playtime skills that will enable them to pursue hobbies as they mature. By providing your children with spaces for doing their various "jobs," you'll also be encouraging them to do their work well and helping them establish good work and play habits. Making sure your children have enough room to work and play doesn't necessarily mean a room for each child. It does mean creating a space that each child can call his or her own, a place to take pride in while doing work to be proud of.

The shared children's rooms pictured on these two pages show how carefully planned work and storage areas provide individual niches for each of the children in a large family. The same principles can be applied on a smaller scale for fewer children, or for one child in a small home.

The room shown *at right* measures 11½x18 feet; it's home to three boys ranging in age from 3 to 10. Because the space is divided by bunk beds and built-in storage units, each boy has his own work/sleep/ play center containing a bed, desk, and dresser. Each has a private place, with room to store books and treasured collectibles.

The picture *below* shows how cozy as well as functional this kind of arrangement can be. It's the sleeping zone of a 13x16-foot room belonging to the boys' three sisters. The

girls range in age from 5 to 12, so privacy is a major concern, as are good lighting and storage.

Having even a small "private" area goes a long way toward giving a child enough room to work. All that's needed is a desk with bookshelves, set off from the rest of the room by a partial divider, such as a dresser, or just the angle of the desk itself.

If bedroom space is really tight, you might consider setting aside a corner of another room, such as the living room or an adult study. You may even find that part of a large closet can be used for more than clothes storage. Equipped with good lighting, a closet can be a fine study nook. For more about setting aside space for children's work, see Chapter 4—"Homework." For help in identifying likely spots for creating children's work centers, see pages 26 and 27.

EVALUATING YOUR NEEDS FOR HOME WORK SPACE

CAN YOU MAKE MONEY WORKING AT HOME?

For many people, making money is an important part of working at home. To some, making money means earning supplemental income for extras and for craft or other specialized supplies; to others, it means a steady and sufficient cash flow that serves as primary or sole financial support. When you consider the pros and cons of working at home, you'll have to consider financial as well as physical and psychological factors.

The sweeping view of woods and fields pictured *at right* may suggest farming rather than inn keeping, but here, an important cash "crop" comes from rooms in the main house and outlying cottages. One cottage is pictured in the inset *opposite, left.* In addition to the view, rustic interiors and colorful country furnishings, shown in the inset photograph *opposite, right,* offer a delightful setting that guests from urban areas are happy to pay for. Although these guesthouses are a labor of love, they more than support themselves. For more about this at-home business, as well as pointers for setting up a guesthouse or inn, see pages 136 and 137.

Any kind of home-based business that involves the sale of goods or services will probably take time to establish. If you're not on salary from an outside source, you're not earning unless your home business is producing income. Can you afford to wait as long as a year for profits?

Consider, too, that some of the activities that lend themselves to working at home, such as writing, editing, and other creative endeavors, are not usually high-profit ventures. Others, such as catering businesses or country inns, are slow-to-build enterprises. In addition, working at home often means working part-time, or starting out at a lower rate of pay to attract customers. Ask yourself whether you hope to earn a living, make a small profit, or just break even while living on another income.

For more about the financial implications of working at home, turn to pages 100-105. For ideas about some intriguing at-home businesses you might not have considered, see Chapter 9.

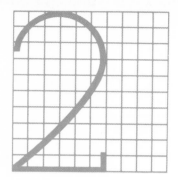

WHERE TO FIND WORK SPACE

If you're seriously considering working at home, whether at your present profession, in a new business venture, or at a space- and time-consuming hobby, finding the right place to work is probably at the top of your priority list. If you have unused and obviously eligible space, such as a dry basement, a clean garage, or a spacious attic, you'll find tips throughout the book on converting these areas for use as work centers. If, however, you don't have any clear-cut candidates for work space and need some inspiration and advice, this chapter will point you in the right direction, then tell what to do when you find the right place.

When you start to think about setting up a place to work at home, first consider several basic points. Perhaps the most important is: Do you need a separate room, or could you share space with other activities? Next, ask yourself how much space you need, in square feet.

Now refine your thinking a little. Ask yourself what *kind* of space you need. Is natural light an amenity or a necessity? What about running water? Should your work space be within easy earshot of household activities, or would detached or sound-insulated quarters be better? Acoustics are especially important if you're involved in musical activity, operate noisy machines, or fear conversation levels might disturb neighbors or family members.

How well-appointed should your workplace be? It should be comfortable, even if you're the only person who spends time there. If outsiders also will use the space, the impression it makes and the convenience of the location and furnishings become increasingly important. In short, do you need to go all out on the design, or will an efficiently set up but low-key back space do?

If you have equipment other than a basic office desk and chair, consider how much space you need for it. In some cases, weight may be a factor, too. Do you need especially strong floors to support any special equipment? Remember, too, that not only do you need room for equipment, you also need room to move around. Be sure the dimensions of your work space allow free passage on all sides of equipment and to stored materials. Also consider the size of

any projects you'll be making. If you're a sculptor or painter, will your works fit through a door or window when it's time to sell or move them?

When you're looking for work space in or around your home, carefully consider its location. If you'll be having visitors, traffic patterns and parking facilities will be important. Consider visitors' convenience, your family's privacy, and neighbors' reactions, even if zoning is not a problem. Plan a separate business visitors' entrance if you'll be conducting a business or a professional practice.

If you'll be generating dirt or debris, locate the work center out of the mainstream of household traffic, so dust and soil don't get tracked in to the rest of the house. Make sure ventilation is adequate, particularly if you'll be working with any sort of chemical.

Electrical needs come into play here, too. A computer, for example, doesn't draw a great deal of current, but the power must be constant and reliable, so the machine ought to be on its own circuit.

A well-planned work space, regardless of size, takes your comfort into account first. Providing enough room and the proper connections or storage places for any tools of the trade is a key to maximizing your own convenience. The spacious crafts room in the drawing *opposite* puts this rule into practice. It's set up as a stained-glass studio. That's a highly specialized use (for more about one practitioner of the art, see pages 130 and 131), but the careful thought and planning that turned a standard basement corner into an efficient and pleasant work center can be applied successfully in many settings for many purposes.

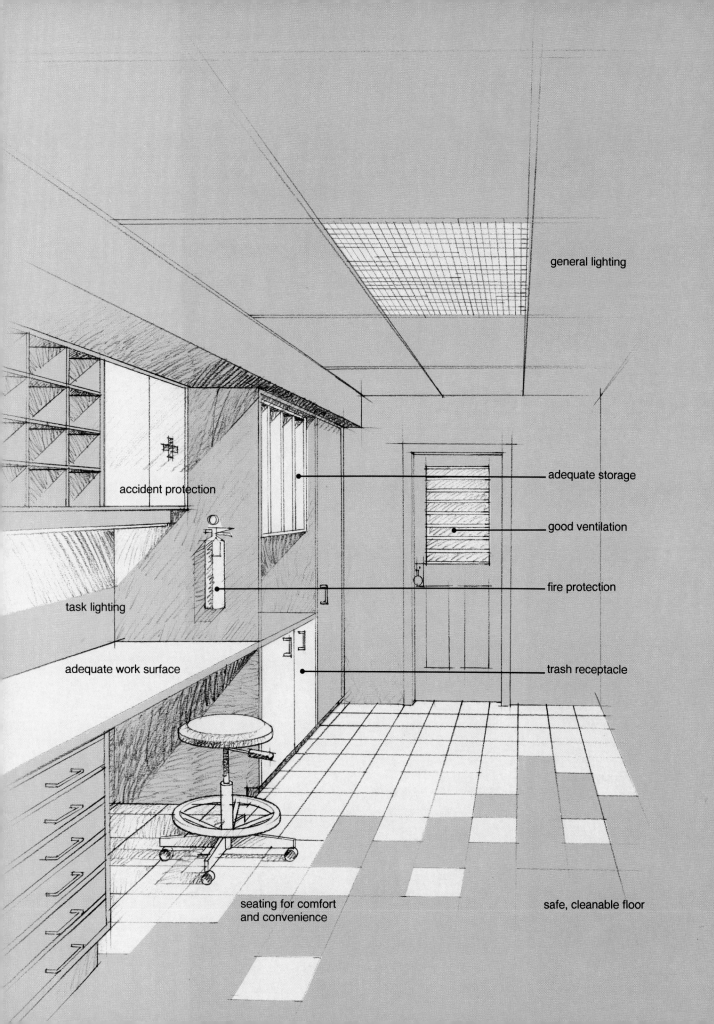

general lighting

adequate storage

accident protection

good ventilation

task lighting

fire protection

adequate work surface

trash receptacle

seating for comfort
and convenience

safe, cleanable floor

SEARCH YOUR HOUSE

Once you've decided how much space you need and what kind it should be, it's time to go hunting. Look at your house, any outbuildings, and surrounding land as if you've never seen them before—or at least been away a long time. Think about every bit of unused or underused space; consider closets, attics, spare rooms, kitchen counters, rarely visited sections of the backyard, the garage you never put your cars in—anything that might be put to better use as a work center.

The schematic drawing *at right* shows a simplified view of a compact one-story house. Although your home probably differs from this one in layout or dimensions, the possibilities outlined may well apply to your house, too.

Working from the outside in

• A house's *perimeter* and yard offer many possibilities. A freestanding greenhouse, for example, opens horizons for a plant enthusiast; a rear bump-out might make the difference between a crowded living room and a new music room for a home-based music teacher.
• The *garage* is an obvious possibility, particularly if you're planning a mechanically oriented activity, such as a woodworking shop. You might set up your work center along one wall, or bump out a wall for additional space. Enclose the work space behind foldaway doors for neatness and privacy. Keep in mind that certain activities that might seem ideal choices for a garage—such as an automotive repair shop—may not be allowed in some residential neighborhoods.
• *Basements* and *attics* also lend themselves to many additional uses. Separated from household activities by stairs and relatively soundproof floors or ceilings, they are rarely used to their fullest capacities. Make sure you have sufficient headroom, however—it's difficult to add height in a basement, though putting a dormer in an attic for extra room and light is a fairly straightforward process.

Shared and borrowed space

• In a *kitchen,* even a small wall area can provide space for a planning or home management center. If your hobby is food related, consider re-outfitting cabinets for more varied storage and use. If you hope to start a food business, you'll have to do more—see pages 134 and 135.
• *Main living areas* can often be converted to part-time office or hobby use. Built-in, purchased, or home-crafted units can give you added work and storage room for your hobby or business—and house everyday items, too. Often, a divider unit can solve the problem of defining living and working space, and help direct traffic.
• *Secondary bedrooms,* whether spare rooms or the rooms of grown-up children, are often perfect spots for activities that need larger or self-enclosed spaces. You may want to consider planning for dual use—using seating that converts to sleeping units, for example—so the guest bedroom function isn't completely lost.
• *Walk-in closets* can quickly convert to office or workshop use. Outfit them carefully, and you'll be able to use every inch of space.
• Also consider using a *corner* or *wall* of a major bedroom as a work or hobby area. Subdivide the space with partial or full walls to further separate sleeping, dressing, and home-office zones.

Build out if you can; free-standing additions are ideal for some purposes, such as greenhouses. And consider bump-outs, too. They add more space than you'd think.

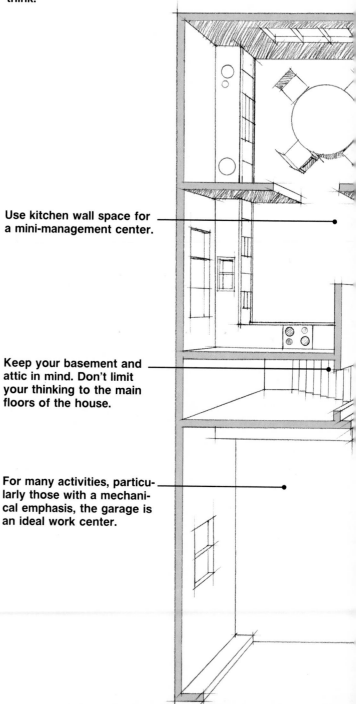

Use kitchen wall space for a mini-management center.

Keep your basement and attic in mind. Don't limit your thinking to the main floors of the house.

For many activities, particularly those with a mechanical emphasis, the garage is an ideal work center.

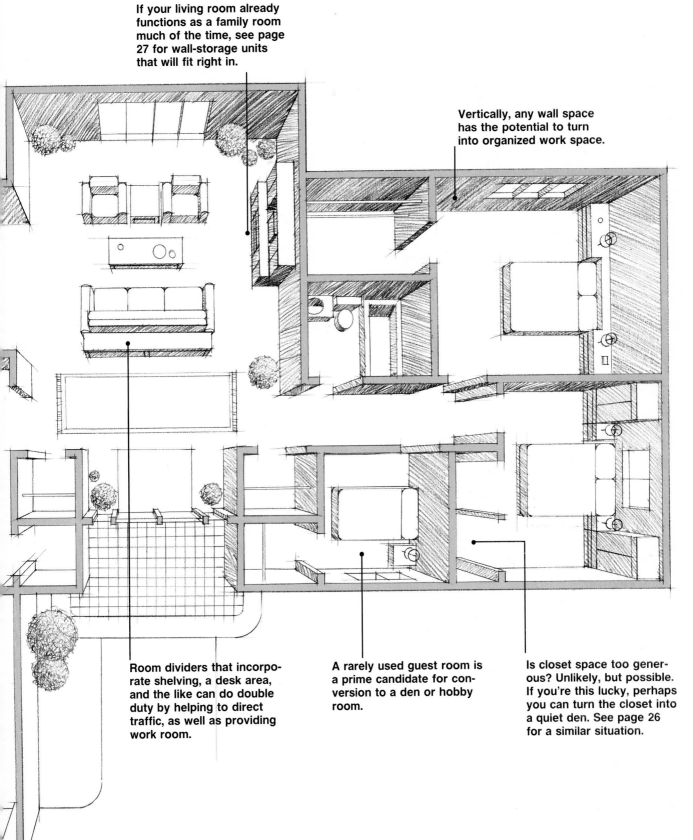

If your living room already functions as a family room much of the time, see page 27 for wall-storage units that will fit right in.

Vertically, any wall space has the potential to turn into organized work space.

Room dividers that incorporate shelving, a desk area, and the like can do double duty by helping to direct traffic, as well as providing work room.

A rarely used guest room is a prime candidate for conversion to a den or hobby room.

Is closet space too generous? Unlikely, but possible. If you're this lucky, perhaps you can turn the closet into a quiet den. See page 26 for a similar situation.

A SMALL-SCALE WORK CENTER

Not only can small be beautiful, it also can be efficient. The trick is not just to find usable space, but to use it to the fullest possible extent. The before and after drawings on these pages show how this can be done.

Bedroom space

The bedroom in the "before" plan *above, right,* provided not only a comfortable place to sleep but also ample clothing storage and a corner desk and chair for doing occasional homework. The room's two functions weren't exactly crowding each other out, but they didn't complement each other, either.

The large plan *below, right,* shows how the same room can be transformed into a real work center, without sacrificing bedroom-style comfort. The bed and night table, in fact, are in just the same location they were in before the transformation.

By reducing the length of the clothes closet, the designer was able to carve a small but complete work center out of a corner previously occupied by the closet. A roll-around chair that tucks into the kneehole corner of the newly added work surface provides greater seating flexibility than the old arrangement did. Bookshelves and a computer counter complete the new "office." In a redo of this kind, it might be necessary to run additional electricity into the new work space to provide for lighting and outlets—usually not a complicated procedure.

The repartitioned closet still provides more-than-adequate clothes storage. With the help of extra rods, other accessories, and perhaps a slightly

deeper design, it would even be possible for the new closet to offer as much hanging room as the original.

Living space

If the work you'd like to carry out in your work center isn't messy or excessively space-greedy, you may be able to give it a home in your living room or family room.

The "before" plan *opposite, above,* shows a standard living room layout, with plenty of

BEFORE

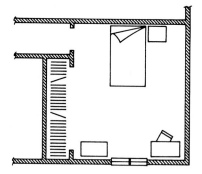

AFTER

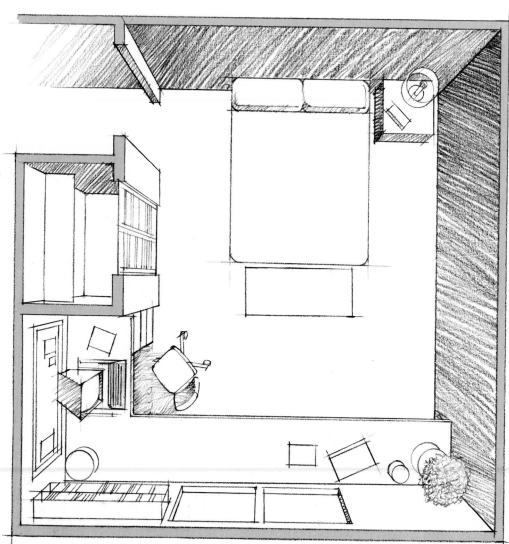

seating but not much storage. Quiet and part-time activities such as sewing, home management, slide viewing, schoolwork, model building, and collection organizing and display particularly lend themselves to sharing work room with living space.

The "after" plan *below* shows several things you can do to create this kind of work space in your home. The flip-down table provides a good work surface, but is barely noticeable when folded back into place. Ample shelving not only handles the books you'd expect to see, but also neatly stores hobby or other materials. Similarly, the doored storage units can hold photo albums, video games, and other everyday items, as well as whatever equipment or materials are needed for the room's work center role. A roll-out extension-style lamp over the worktable would provide serviceable task lighting.

BEFORE

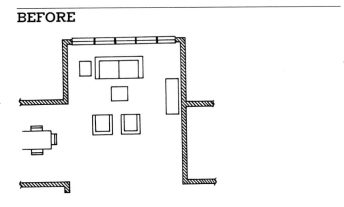

AFTER

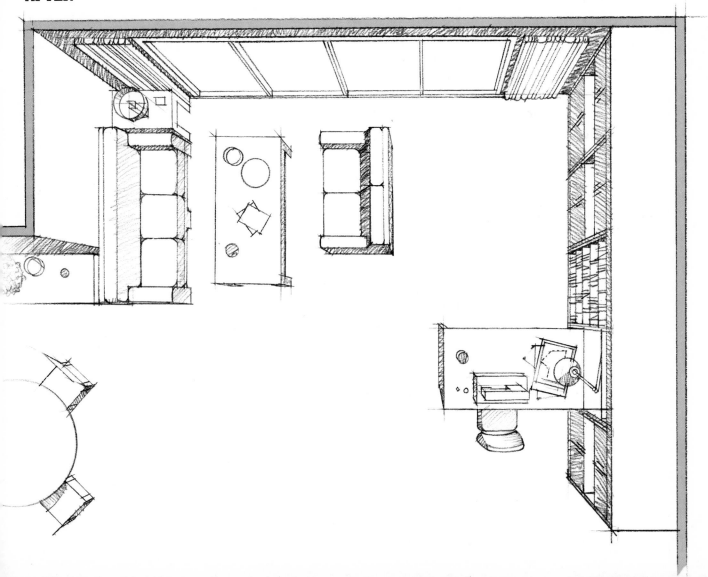

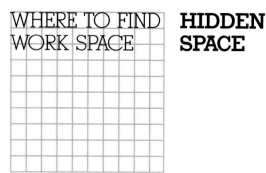

HIDDEN SPACE

BASEMENT ROOM

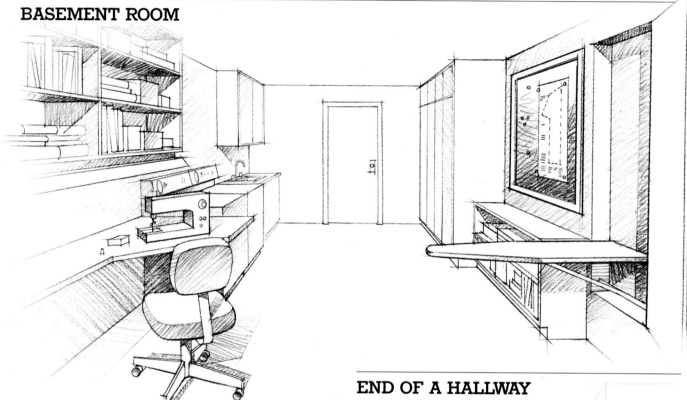

Hidden space doesn't have to be mysterious; it isn't necessarily behind secret doors, in the darkest part of your attic, or in a remote corner of your yard. It is, however, likely to be space you didn't think could be put to good use, because it seems too small or too inaccessible, or is being used for other purposes.

Here, two walls have been equipped with the necessary equipment. The sewing machine has a permanent position on a newly built work counter, which also doubles as desk space. There's ample room for a chair anywhere along the counter.

Directly opposite the sewing machine, a fold-down ironing board is handy for both newly finished items and just-laundered ones. Pattern pinup space and generous storage for fabric, notions, and patterns complete the work center. The sink, dryer, and washing machine line up along the wall beyond the sewing area.

Dead space
The end of a hallway is usually a dead end, but if you've been searching for a place to put a mini-office, the space may be ripe for a quick revival. In the drawing *at right,* a 4-foot-wide niche beyond the last doorway in a corridor has been turned into a compact work zone. A side-mounted wall fixture provides sufficient light for reading and writing. High wall-mounted storage cabinets conceal papers and notebooks; bookshelves below provide not only practical storage but room for a few small decorative items, too. The

END OF A HALLWAY

distance between the desk top and the shelves is just enough for a word processor. Placing file drawers against the wall helps support the desk top and leaves a little extra legroom. Because this work space is both small and visible from the main living area of the home, choosing a small and attractive chair would be more important than simply finding one that rolls on casters.

Garage space

You may really need most of your garage space for your cars, at least during cold or snowy seasons. All the same, you can probably develop a good workshop/storage section along the far wall. By mounting storage cabinets or shelves for tools and chemicals in double tiers, you get more use from less wall space. In the drawing *at upper right,* note the niche left below one set of cabinets. It provides accessible storage for spare tires, hoses, and other bulky items that would otherwise take up more than their share of floor space.

A quiet corner

Corners often offer limited wall space because they're close to doors or windows. For that reason, they aren't always used to their greatest potential—or to any potential. By choosing desk and storage space carefully, you may be able to put a corner of virtually any room to work as a quiet-time work "room." The drawing *at lower right* shows how an L-shape desk combines forces with a deep, wall-hung cabinet and unobtrusive articulated desk lamp to turn wasted space into a compact, productive work zone.

END WALL OF A GARAGE

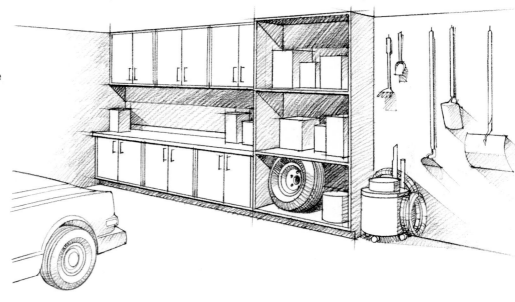

AN UNUSED CORNER

29

A DUAL-PURPOSE ROOM

You may already have created an informal, unofficial dual-purpose room simply by setting up your home management center in the kitchen, or squeezing a drawing board, clamp-on light, and stool into your den. With careful planning and special furnishings, you can take double-duty space several steps beyond that.

A darkroom/guest bedroom

If you have a spare bedroom, even a very small one, your home is always ready to provide a gracious welcome to overnight visitors. You may hesitate to sacrifice hospitality for the sake of a workroom—and, in fact, you don't need to.

The drawings on these pages show how a standard-issue spare room can double as an efficient, well-equipped, and somewhat unconventional darkroom. By turning two corners of the room into enclosed work areas, the designer created an entrance corridor leading to the sleeping section of the room. The room's window is at the far end, eliminating the problem of natural light in the darkrooms and maximizing its effect where it's most welcome—in the open part of the room.

As the drawings indicate, this darkroom has a dry side and a wet side. The wet side, detailed *opposite,* is next to a bathroom, simplifying plumbing connections. Here, a sink, counter, storage, and safelight provide all the essentials for developing film and washing prints. A ventilator, tapped into ductwork for the bath, carries away chemical fumes.

The dry side, shown *below* and *at near right,* was created by opening up a walk-in closet

DRY SIDE

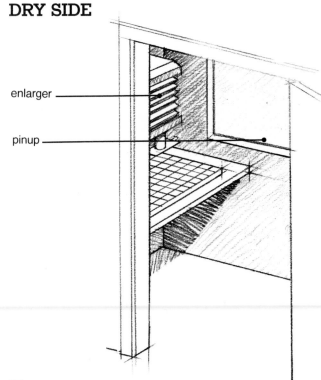

enlarger

pinup

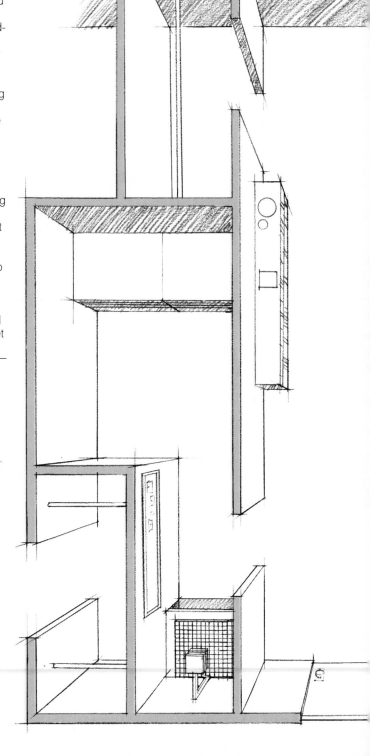

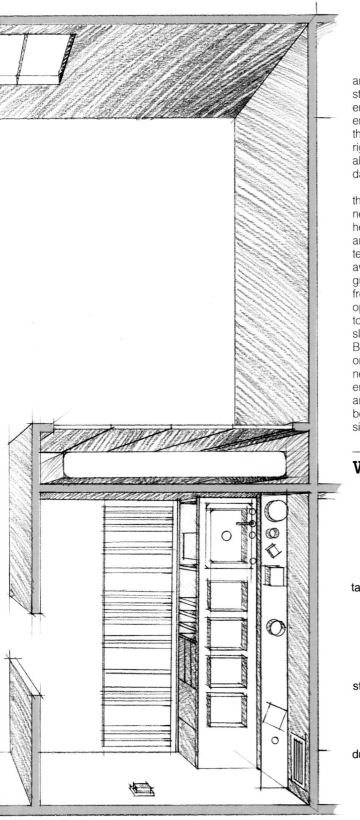

and building a new wall that steals a couple of feet from the end of the room. The new wall encloses a niche adjacent to the former closet that's just right for an enlarger. (For more about setting up your own darkroom, see pages 66-69.)

Both sections are entered through doors just inside the new entrance corridor; this helps maintain a sense of separateness in the guest quarters. Here, a Murphy bed folds away during the day and when guests are not in residence, freeing floor space. The bed opens easily and quickly to provide comfortable guest sleeping accommodations. Because the room has lost its original closet, new storage is needed. A storage unit at the end of the new wall provides ample room for guests' belongings and family possessions, including cameras.

Other ways to maximize space

Not every hobby or work space requires this much construction to fit it into a room that's already serving another purpose. In many cases, all that's needed are specialized furnishings and storage units. Items such as closet accessories, wire-grid bins that hook to desk tops, fold-down shelves, and drop-leaf tables offer ways to almost instantly reorganize a room.

To provide guest sleeping facilities in a dual-purpose room, consider innovative furnishings such as hinged-top end tables that quickly convert to single beds and fabric-covered tables that conceal double-width ottomans—which pull open to form double beds. These and other furnishings and accessories can turn virtually any room into two.

WET SIDE

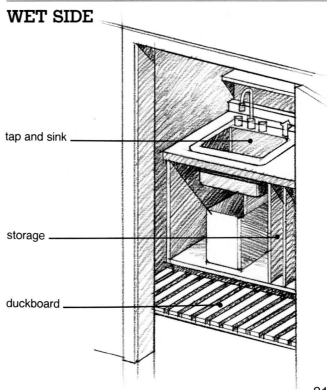

tap and sink

storage

duckboard

A WORK-CENTERED ADDITION

Adding on to your home is not a project to be undertaken lightly, nor is it an option to dismiss out of hand. If you're happy with your home but need room for a hobby, craft, or at-home business, an addition might be just the way to go. The key is to plan new space that can accommodate your need for work room now, yet be easily converted to less specialized uses later.

For example, the addition pictured here is outfitted to serve as a potter's studio, complete with running water, ample electricity, and abundant natural light. Move out the kiln, potters wheel, and other ceramics equipment, and the space could just as easily serve as a commodious family room or master suite arrayed around a window-flanked fireplace. A strategically placed skylight and a wood floor would work as well in a general-purpose room as in a work space.

When you plan an addition, always consider how it will fit into your home's existing traffic patterns and how it will affect your home's exterior appearance. In this case, both concerns were addressed early, and the results reflect that, as the small drawing *opposite* and the plan *below* both illustrate.

The extension, added at the rear, is accessible from both the family room and the garage; it's conveniently close to existing plumbing and other utility lines. In an outdoor niche formed between the addition and one of the original walls, there's a new, sheltered deck. A vertical-sided exterior, visible to family members and neighbors, provides a dramatic contemporary accent for the otherwise conventionally styled clapboard ranch house.

To learn more about pottery studios, see pages 74-75 and 80-81; to look at another addition, this one a woodworking shop that can easily convert to a family room, turn to pages 86 and 87.

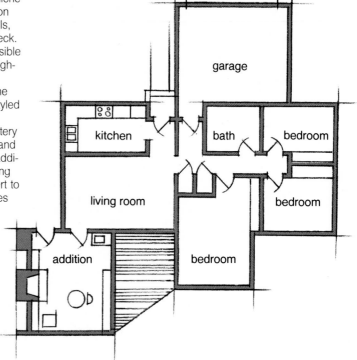

If you decide to add on, you may want to tailor your new space to work center use, yet keep it flexible enough to convert easily to a more general purpose in the future. Some day, for example, a potter's studio might serve equally well as a family room. Natural light, surface treatments, and traffic patterns should be planned with later conversion in mind.

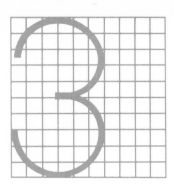

HOME MANAGEMENT CENTERS

Home management is an impressive-sounding task that virtually everyone does, although not everyone thinks about the minutiae of running a household in such formal terms. No matter how small your home or how flexible your routine, you almost certainly compose shopping lists, schedule events, and keep track of maintenance needs. The list-making may be on handy scraps of paper and the event-scheduling in a tattered wallet-size notebook, but the goal is household management. In this chapter you'll find planning and work centers that can help you organize and streamline your own home management chores.

PLANNING CENTERS: WHAT TO INCLUDE

Good planning alone won't keep your household running smoothly, but it will give you a start in the right direction. As with most other jobs, once you know what has to be done, and when, the actual work seems both more logical and less intimidating.

The planning center pictured here occupies one wall of a spacious kitchen—a sensible arrangement if your kitchen is large enough to accommodate an extra feature. Just about any spare corner or "dead" wall space, however, can become a serviceable planning center. The key ingredients are a writing surface, a storage drawer, a comfortable place to sit, and time to think. Any spot that's convenient and allows you a few minutes of peace and quiet will do fine.

The scientific approach
The planning center pictured *here* is so efficiently designed that it almost looks suitable for scientific research. More important, you really can do a lot of careful planning here. The clean-lined, laminate-covered counters and drawers offer ample writing and storage space. The chair is a classic office-desk model that takes up little room. Thanks to a hinged flip-up countertop, the typewriter, permanently nestled between two counter/drawer sections, can be stored instantly and covered by additional counter space.

Everything here is designed to work smoothly. Surfaces are easy to maintain, accessories such as a telephone and memo pad are right at hand, and views through the large-paned windows make even routine tasks pleasant.

KITCHEN PLANNING CENTERS

Just as the kitchen is the heart of many homes, kitchen-oriented planning is the core of home management in many households. Much kitchen planning focuses on food: preparation, storage, purchasing, and eating. It also encompasses a whole range of food-related activities, from the enjoyable (entertaining) to the functional (appliance maintenance). All of these activities can find a place in a well-planned kitchen planning center.

Certainly there's no rule against jotting things down in a little notebook that travels with you. If you want to make home planning into domestic science, however, the best place to organize priorities and make lists is right where the plans will be carried out.

Just what you want from your kitchen planning center depends mostly on the amount of cooking and food-buying you do, the number of people involved in your plans, and the amount of space you have. A few features are vital, however—counter space, something to sit on, and writing paper and pens. A telephone and a calendar come in handy, too.

Your primary kitchen planning task is probably keeping track of food and cleaning supplies. A center near the refrigerator, food cupboards, and cleaning supply areas is ideal. Having your cookbooks handy, as they are in both of the planning centers shown here, is an added advantage. With recipes in easy reach and all in one place, it's easier to sit down and plan meals that use what's in the house, as well as plan company menus.

When you're busy in the kitchen, you may see the telephone as a disruption. But if you've set aside a time and place to organize shopping lists, dentist appointments, and car pool schedules, having a phone at hand saves time and steps. And if you're up to your elbows in bread dough, or right in the middle of preparing a meal where timing is critical, it's especially handy to have a phone within reach. If that phone is a speaker phone, you can continue with the bread or dinner and converse at the same time.

Adult family members may have favorite decorative desk calendars, and teenagers may jealously guard their daily diaries from public view, but a primary calendar can help pull everyone's activities together.

The two kitchen planning centers pictured here are unobtrusive, practical, and attractive. The lacquered-pine, cantilevered desk shown *below* is 3½ feet high, so you can use it sitting on a standard bar stool or standing up. A notch at the rear accommodates the cord from a standard desk phone. At left, French doors and a window bring in light; above, track lights provide nighttime illumination.

The planning center pictured *opposite* combines antique charm with modern function. The oak pedestal-style desk, with its white plastic-laminate top, is new; the desk chair and a small file cabinet at right are antiques. Shelves (not shown) to the left of the ovens hold cookbooks.

CENTERS IN OTHER AREAS

Home management is more than planning. It's also a matter of keeping things in good repair and running smoothly. That covers just about everything from sewing on loose buttons to making sure bills are paid on time. The specifics of furnishing your center will vary with the activities you want it to handle, but desk or counter space, well-thought-out though not necessarily standard storage, and a comfortable place to sit are essential.

The many-faceted home management center pictured *opposite* and *at lower right* serves as a household office, kitchen-storage center, and scullery. Long ago, it was a butler's pantry; now, all members of the household use it for a wide range of planning and home management activities.

The handsome wood wall unit featured *opposite* holds files, financial records, and other vital "business" materials. Above is a combination of open shelving, glass-front cabinets, and four shallow file drawers. Small drawers below desktop hold sewing and mending supplies so that any family member can find the means to sew on a button or strengthen a seam as the need arises. The typewriter, telephone, and calculator serve as homework aids, as well as home management tools.

Across the room, in the area shown *at right,* things are less businesslike. A pass-through below the dish shelves links the counter to the kitchen. When the family entertains, they use this area for buffet and drink service, and for cleanup afterward. An auxiliary dishwasher, here, is located conveniently close to storage for party dishes.

The lighting in the two separate areas of this management center is tailored to the purpose each zone serves. Overhead lights down the center provide adequate general illumination—supplemented, it's important to note, by task lighting. On both sides of the room

fluorescent fixtures tuck beneath the shelves.

Variations of a theme
No two households or families are exactly alike, but there are some tasks just about everyone has to tackle. For example, when you think of running a household, you probably think of keeping track of your family's financial obligations, keeping up with social and other correspondence, and keeping clothes clean, ironed, and in good condition. If you are active in community or other organizations, the telephoning and record keeping required by that activity may

very well be done in the same place you use for family business.

If one or more of these household management activities take up a large proportion of your time, you may wish you could devote a corresponding amount of space to it, as well. For example, the office/homework wall pictured *opposite* could be set up to meet needs somewhat different from those it now handles, and the "active" side of the room shown *below* could become a laundry/sewing area. The counter might be used as a sewing table, with a washer and dryer built in underneath.

PLANNING FOR A HOME COMPUTER

Computers were once the wave of the future. Now, it seems the future is here. Computers are familiar fixtures in the workplace, and are becoming increasingly so in the home, as well. Finding room in your house for a computer is not a mystical process, although it does take some planning. On this and the following three pages, we'll give you some tips on living and working comfortably with a home computer.

Home computers got their start as entertainment accessories; teenagers and their younger siblings have grown up with video games. Computers are still fun, but in the past few years, they've moved out of the TV room and into the den, kitchen, and family room. Computers now help with such routine and once time-consuming household chores as budgeting, recording and filing bill payments and addresses, writing letters, and more.

Beyond making home management more efficient, computers can link the conventional workplace to the home, and in some cases turn home into a workplace. Taking work home or working at home regularly isn't a matter of bulging briefcases anymore; instead, it often means a computer network linking places that may be thousands of miles apart.

Learning the language

Computer terminology, like any specialized language, takes getting used to, but the language of electronics isn't difficult to learn. If you are planning to purchase a computer, you'll want to talk in detail to sales personnel at reputable computer stores: Find out what a given model can do, to what extent it can *interface,* or interact, with other computers, and what software is available. You'll need a passing acquaintance with computer language to get the conversation started, though.

Computer parts are either *hardware* or *software.* Hardware is the machinery itself; software is the informational material, or *program,* that plugs into the hardware.

A standard computer system has two primary hardware components.

• The *keyboard console* is the part that looks like a typewriter. It often contains the *central processing unit* (CPU), which does the actual work. The console is where you enter commands.

• The *monitor* is the part that looks like a television screen. This is where the computer displays information, in words, graphs, or pictures.

Software, the heart of the computer, comes in three forms: cartridge, cassette tape, and disk. *Cartridges* plug into the computer console; they are the easiest type of software to use, but they do not store information in the computer, and are not sophisticated programming devices. *Cassettes* look like audio tape cassettes, and some are the same as the ones used in standard cassette players. Cassettes hold longer programs than cartridges do, but are slow to transfer information, and don't always operate smoothly. They may become obsolete shortly. *Disks,* also known as floppy diskettes, store a considerable amount of information and transfer instructions to the computer very quickly. Sophisticated programs are usually on disks.

To transfer instructions from a disk to a computer, you'll most likely need a *disk drive,* which performs much the same job as a record player. Some more expensive computers have drives built into the console, but usually the drive is a separate element.

If you want to link your computer to the outside world, you'll need a *modem,* a box-like device that transmits and receives information over telephone lines. There are social computer networks and informational networks that charge for time spent on the line. And, more and more, businesses are linking their office computer systems to employees' homes, turning them into the "electronic cottages" that once seemed so futuristic.

A *printer* puts electronic information onto paper. This is an optional component, but one you'll require for word processing. If you're a writer or editor, or hope your children will do much of their homework on the computer, this is a key but somewhat costly item.

How smart does your computer have to be?

Software for home computers is being developed in great quantity and at surprising speed. You should be able to do more with your computer a year from now than you originally planned. How much memory your computer has is a key to how much you can expand it. Many of the less expensive computers have only a 16K memory, meaning they hold 16,000 bytes, or letters. This is fairly limited, but you can buy add-on memory modules. More expensive home computers may hold up to 128K, more than adequate for most household tasks.

Finding a home for your home computer

To make sure you use a computer to its fullest potential, you'll need to find a location for it that's convenient for all members of your family. The model shown here is tucked under a television set in a kitchen planning center, but that's just one possibility.

Keep in mind that the assorted components may be visually distracting if they're placed in your living room. And if some family members are likely to use the computer at odd hours, keeping it away from sleeping zones is a good idea.

(continued)

PLANNING FOR
A HOME COMPUTER
(continued)

Whether you expect your home computer to be primarily a study tool for youngsters, a working-at-home asset for adults, or a household management assistant, the physical conditions under which you and the computer work are very important.

Two basic computer needs must be met right away. First, keep in mind that steady electrical power is very important for computers. Sudden surges can erase a computer's memory or scramble the work you're doing. Put the computer on its own circuit to avoid damage from power surges caused by appliances in your home. To protect the computer from problems caused by external electrical disturbances, consider buying a surge arrester or power line filter, available at computer stores or through the mail.

Second, good telephone service is vital if you plan to use the computer with a modem. You may want to get a separate telephone line for transmitting and receiving information. This enables you to talk to the outside world while the computer is on its own.

Good working conditions for people, too

Ergonomics is the term for the science of designing and arranging spaces so that people and furnishings (or machines) interact efficiently, comfortably, and safely. The more technology advances, the more important this people-oriented science becomes.

The room shown *at right* was designed as a learning center for teenage members of a family; the principles it illustrates apply to just about any work center that includes a computer among its components.

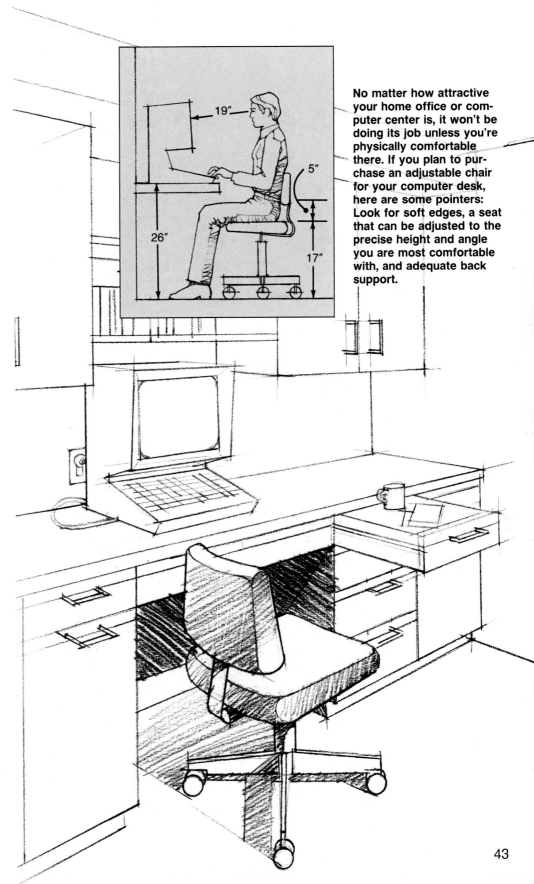

• The *work surface* is matte-finish plastic laminate, chosen to prevent glare. An abundance of counter space allows each part of the computer its own turf. Many manufacturers produce desks specifically designed for computers, but any solid counter, desk, or typing table will do.

• *Shelving* is designed to hold considerable weight—in this case, both books and a large amount of software.

• *Seating,* as for any workplace, is comfortable and functional. The chair is designed to prevent back fatigue and has antistatic nylon upholstery; avoiding static is especially important when you're using a computer. Broad rollers on the chair make it easy to move from one part of the counter to another as tasks change.

• *Lighting* was chosen for its nonglare qualities. Task lighting mounted directly below the shelves brightens the area immediately surrounding the computer.

• *Antistatic carpeting* or other static-retarding flooring is important for any room in which a computer will be used. This carpet is also practical because it has short, dense pile that chairs can roll over easily.

• *Wall covering* in this room is acoustical material. You'll especially want sound-muffling qualities if your computer will be in use when some family members are asleep. Many acoustical wallcoverings have the added advantage of being soft enough to double as bulletin boards.

The large illustration in the box at right shows in schematic form the features you need to look and plan for before you set up a home computer center. The smaller drawing indicates the space requirements for an average-size computer user at a standard terminal.

No matter how attractive your home office or computer center is, it won't be doing its job unless you're physically comfortable there. If you plan to purchase an adjustable chair for your computer desk, here are some pointers: Look for soft edges, a seat that can be adjusted to the precise height and angle you are most comfortable with, and adequate back support.

PLANNING A HOME MANAGEMENT CENTER

The illustration *at right* includes almost everything the most ambitious home manager might want in a work center: ample storage, work space, and specialized equipment. Your needs may be less varied, or your space and resources more limited than those envisioned here. Use this model to select the features that would be the most helpful for you.

• *Storage.* The closed cabinets above the counter are for materials that won't be needed often but must be reasonably accessible. Open shelving below the cabinets is ideal for books and other frequently used materials. The counter-level storage provides privacy and easy accessibility for financial records. Across the room, open storage accommodates anything from children's art supplies to back issues of periodicals. The fireproof files keep hard-to-replace papers safe, but very valuable items might be better stored in a bank box or home safe.

• *Work space.* The sturdy counter can hold a typewriter or computer; the chair is comfortable for any desk activity. Overhead task lighting can be adjusted to fit each type of work done at the desk. A bulletin board above the counter keeps family members' ongoing projects in sight and mind. Carpeting in this part of the center has several purposes: Besides being nice to look at and pleasant to the touch, it muffles sounds.

This home management center incorporates a specialized workroom, focusing on laundry and clothes care. Here, resilient flooring makes for easy maintenance; you could use cushioned resilient flooring for better sound insulation. Natural lighting from the large window is a plus.

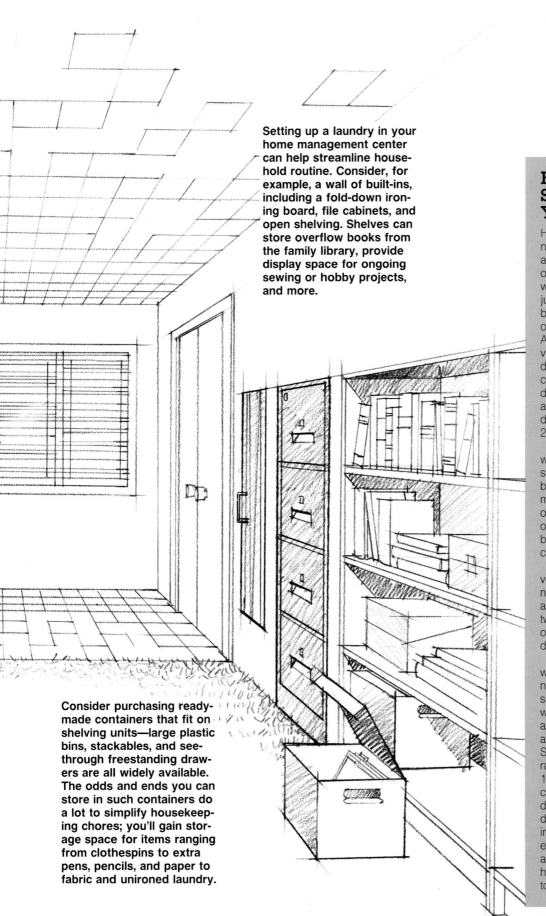

Setting up a laundry in your home management center can help streamline household routine. Consider, for example, a wall of built-ins, including a fold-down ironing board, file cabinets, and open shelving. Shelves can store overflow books from the family library, provide display space for ongoing sewing or hobby projects, and more.

Consider purchasing ready-made containers that fit on shelving units—large plastic bins, stackables, and see-through freestanding drawers are all widely available. The odds and ends you can store in such containers do a lot to simplify housekeeping chores; you'll gain storage space for items ranging from clothespins to extra pens, pencils, and paper to fabric and unironed laundry.

HOW MUCH SPACE DO YOU NEED?

How much space you need in your home management center depends on how many items you want to include. If you just need a desk or table and chair, a couple of square yards will do. Although desk area can vary greatly, a writing desk's height should be close to the office standard of 29 to 30 inches; a typewriter or computer desk should be about 26 inches high.

Computers and typewriters don't come in a single size. Before you buy a desk or table, measure *your* typewriter or computer, not someone else's, and remember to account for the carriage return, if any.

If you want a more versatile center, space needs increase. For example, you will need between 48 and 56 inches of wall space for a standard laundry center.

Prebuilt shelf units, which you'll probably need, take up wall space, but come in a wide range of widths and heights, starting at about 18x30 inches. Shelf depth usually ranges from 8 inches to 12 or 13 inches. File cabinets are more standardized. Letter-size file drawers measure 15 inches wide by 29 inches deep; legal-size files are 3 inches wider. Unit heights range from two to five drawers.

4

HOMEWORK

For some of us, the line between home and office is blurring. Demanding jobs require many people to bring work home in the evenings or on weekends. Others moonlight at a second job out of their home. Used only part-time, space for a small study or work center often can be created in rooms such as bedrooms, living rooms, or even hallways that are traditionally reserved for other functions. Just be sure that the two uses are compatible. A night-owl workaholic, for example, may not be welcome in a shared bedroom.

With the growing number of two-income families, the need for dual-purpose work areas is also on the rise. No matter how loving a relationship is, however, a shared work space can be fraught with problems. Who has first right to the area? What if work materials are incompatible—a "messy" craft versus a "neat" profession? Even if used at different times of day, a shared work station necessitates an endless round of cleanup. Work in progress must constantly be stashed to free the area for the other worker. Supplies also must be accommodated.

These problems are not insurmountable, however. As this little study for two proves, what counts is not how big but how carefully conceived a work space is. A tiny room can yield ample work and storage areas for two separate but simultaneous tasks.

The solution pictured in the photo *at left* is a simple built-in desk and work surface with storage and task areas custom-designed for two different workers.

The architect/stained-glass hobbyist's work area is at left, a sewing area for his spouse is at right. Between the two, a bank of wide, shallow drawers serves both—ideal for stowing fabrics, architectural drawings, and supplies.

A wall-hung bookcase running the length of one wall offers plenty of open-shelf storage for books and baskets of craft supplies; antique drawer units store small items.

French doors flood the small room with natural light that's augmented by ample built-in general and task lighting. White walls brighten and enlarge the space, and a polyurethane finish protects the oak floor.

A STUDY OFF THE BEDROOM

For a private retreat from the mainstream of family commotion, consider creating a study off the bedroom. Although not without some drawbacks, this location could be ideal for daytime or weekend use. Removed from household distractions, it offers a quiet hideaway for reading, writing, or creative work. If you plan to work late at night or early in the morning, however, another location where you're less likely to disturb a sleeping spouse might be more appropriate.

To keep office clutter from intruding on the bedroom, define the office as a separate entity, both functionally and visually. As this remodeling shows, a little foresight can help head off any conflicts of interest between bedroom and office functions.

Here, a separate office was created by designing a room within a room. Although quite small, the office does not feel claustrophobic, thanks to abundant wall cutouts and an arched window. Instead of a cramped cubbyhole, this very small space became an open and inviting, but separate, work space adjoining the master bedroom.

Raising the level of the office above the adjoining bedroom by three steps also helped define the work center without any need for solid wall partitions.

Separate lighting, storage, and work surfaces also keep an office from usurping part of the bedroom and help it to function more efficiently.

In this remodeling, strategically placed task lighting permits occasional nighttime use of the study without unwelcome light shining into the sleeping area.

As the floor plan below illustrates, well-planned built-ins can alleviate crowded floor space. Custom-designed U-shape cabinetry features a curved desk-cabinet that flows along three walls, making efficient use of every inch of the room.

office

bedroom

A STUDY
IN THE
LIVING ROOM

In a small home or apartment, every room must pull its weight. Even the living room must be more than just a showplace for company. Though traditionalists may balk at setting up shop in the living room, this remodeling makes a now-you-see-it, now-you-don't case for creative and efficient space planning.

When the owners purchased their 1,600-square-foot, two-bedroom-plus-family-room condominium, they were immediately faced with a tough space planning decision: how to provide bedrooms for their son and daughter, and an office for an executive who frequently works at home. The ingeniously designed built-in unit shown here solves both problems.

Previously, an opening to the right of the fireplace, shown *below*, connected the living and family rooms. The owners filled the opening with a divider—a box that's free-standing except for lateral bracing. Behind the divider, the former family room now serves as a bedroom that easily can be converted to family room use later.

On the living room side, shutter doors conceal the compact and efficient office and entertainment center shown *opposite*. In a unit that's just 2 feet deep, the designers found space for a television set and stereo gear, records, file drawers, a worktable, and ample open-shelf storage for books and office supplies.

The drop-down worktable is attached at the bottom by piano hinges. Folded up, it conceals the storage areas. Lighting includes a fluorescent fixture under the bottom shelf and a flex-arm incandescent lamp.

On the other side of the divider (not shown), a closet and bulletin board serve the new bedroom.

SMALL SPACE STUDIES

Small can be beautiful, and efficient, too, when a pint-size space is given a big, well-thought-out design. Making the most of a small area takes extra effort, but thorough planning and careful selection of furniture can keep a tiny work center from looking cramped and cluttered.

Room for a home office for two was found in a narrow area adjoining the master bedroom, shown *at right*. The inexpensive desks beneath the windows are simple laminate-top counters resting on file cabinets. A bank of closets and upper cabinets built along a blank wall provides ample storage space to handle both office supplies and clothing.

Supplementing the natural light from the windows, two desk lights give needed illumination to each work space.

A compact corner

Tucked under the eaves in a tight corner, the grouping pictured *opposite* takes advantage of every inch of available space. Programmed to lead more than one life, this arrangement combines a work center, hobby area, and dining spot in one streamlined unit.

By selecting multipurpose pieces like these, you can make your furniture dollars as well as your space go further. Two tall cabinets, side by side, house all the supplies needed for a home office. Unsightly gear disappears behind the cabinet doors, and open shelves store books and *objets d'art*. A bank of low, wall-hugging drawers and cabinets provides more stashing space where headroom is minimal. The sleek desk top can be extended from 68 to 84 inches to spread out work or to accommodate more seating for impromptu dining or games.

STUDIES IN CLOSETS

Are you a closet executive? If so, you're in good company. More and more homeowners and apartment dwellers are eyeing closet space as possibilities for compact homework centers.

Any closet can be converted easily from garment storage to a compact office away from the office. Generally about two feet deep, closet recesses offer ideal proportions for adding shelves and a work surface. To incorporate a new study into the room, just remove the existing closet doors. If you prefer to hide clutter from sight when the study is not in use, install bifold or shutter doors.

Created in the mini-space a 3-foot-wide closet once occupied, the tiny study shown *opposite* and *below* is the picture of efficiency. A do-it-yourself project, this conversion conserves materials as well as space. Just one sheet of ¾-inch plywood yielded all the shelving. A piano hinge installed on the wall side of the desk lets the surface adjust to lie flat or tilt as a drawing board. A strip of 1¾-inch screen molding acts as a

pencil stop. For a handsome, finished appearance, you could build a similar unit of oak or ash plywood. Or, use a less expensive grade of plywood, and paint or laminate it.

For extra storage, a rolling taboret handles small, miscellaneous items; above the desk is a handy bulletin board.

In tight quarters like this, a mirrored wall works wonders by creating the illusion of spaciousness. If you enjoy background music while you work, select micro stereo components and speakers.

Another example of an efficient mini-study carved from a petite-size closet, the work center pictured *at right* relies on a series of open shelves supported by L-brackets and lined with colorful, inexpensive plastic bins that handle miscellaneous paraphernalia. For less carpentry work, purchase stackable bins and set them on one or two shelves. Covered with cork, the adjoining wall makes a nifty bulletin board for a calendar, notes, and doodles. A wall-hung light and rolling chair were the only other accessories needed to outfit this office.

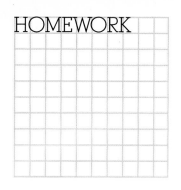

KIDS' HOMEWORK SPACES

Homework may seem less of a chore for children who have comfortable, attractive work places. Ideally, at school age every child should have a special place of his own to study, read, draw, work on projects, or just daydream.

A child's work center should be scaled to kid-size. Putting everything within a child's limited reach encourages independence and frees Mom and Dad from constant pleas for help.

Adequate storage is a top priority for kids' spaces. There should be low shelves for toys and games, drawers and cabinets for closed storage, and a desk with ample room for projects, books, and supplies.

Whether you purchase ready-made furniture or select built-ins, plan for growth. Look for designs that feature adjustable heights. Many of the chairs, tables, and desks now available can be raised as the child grows. If you're building your own, allow for later adjustments. (For specifics, see the box below.)

A bright, cheerful, but simple decorating theme works best for children of all ages. Select colors and furnishings that won't seem babyish in a few years. And beware of spending a lot of money on decorating that will soon seem passé. Your little one may adore teddy bears now, but he may soon prefer race cars and spacemen.

The child's work space shown *at right* has all the features big people want in a work space, but on a lilliputian scale. Light colors, lots of smooth surfaces and concealed storage, and an emphasis on long, horizontal lines make the small space look larger than it really is.

The built-in desk features a laminate-covered desk top trimmed in oak. There's ample storage for school supplies in the bin drawers (see inset photo). Their curved design keeps the area below free for play or for knee space when the desk is used.

Fluorescent under-cabinet lights help prevent strain on young eyes. Cabinets are mounted low for easy access and give extra storage above. The chair seat can be adjusted and the entire work surface can be remounted higher as the child grows.

PLANNING FOR GROWTH

Kids' furniture purchased ready-made should meet the following size guidelines. Standard height for a desk is 22 inches, with 26 inches of knee space. Chairs should be 20 inches from floor to seat, 24 inches wide, and 16 inches deep. A small worktable should be 23 inches high, 31 inches wide, and 23 inches deep.

If you plan to build furniture for children, recommended heights by age group for chairs and tables are:

Age	1-4	5-7	8-10	11-14
Chair Seat	12″	12-14″	13-17″	15-18″
Table	18″	20-24″	24-27″	26-30″

PLANNING STUDY SPACES

Whether you tuck your study into a tiny closet or devote an entire room to it, planning for comfort and efficiency is essential.

The generic work center illustrated here suggests ideas you can incorporate in your own retreat. The basics of any work space include adequate and convenient storage, good lighting, work surfaces, and seating.

A study should be large enough to meet your equipment and storage needs but small enough to be snug and inviting. Although it need not be totally isolated, select a reasonably quiet and distraction-free zone if you can.

The work surface should be generous, with a firm, rugged, and easily cleaned finish. If you use a typewriter, install a nonskid surface to keep the machine in place. A surface slightly lower than the rest of the counter is most comfortable for typing. If the carriage moves, allow adequate space for operation.

Storage needs vary, but few of us ever complain about having too much of it. Include both open and auxiliary closed storage areas, plus lockable file cabinets and drawers, if needed.

Flooring can be any comfortable, attractive material, but a tiled area next to the desk will help the chair roll easily and will make cleanup simpler.

Good back and leg support is mandatory for a desk chair. A swivel chair that can be adjusted in height is a worthwhile extra. Business and pleasure can mix, so if space and budget permit, comfortable seating for relaxation is a bonus.

Don't overlook ventilation, both for heating and for cooling. If necessary, add a window or open a wall to adjacent space to improve airflow.

When you're considering how to arrange a study space, take some cues from efficient kitchen design. A U- or L-shape layout keeps work stations close together and, combined with a rolling office chair, minimizes footsteps. In the drawing below, a desk and typing table form one side of an L; a long table with a wide work surface, the other.

LIGHTING NEEDS

Good lighting is a necessity, not a luxury. Locate fixtures properly and choose the correct bulb or tube to avoid eyestrain and fatigue.

For *general lighting*, use table lamps, wall- or ceiling-mounted fixtures, or recessed or track lighting.

In a study space of 150 square feet or less, plan on a three- to five-socket incandescent *ceiling fixture* with a total of 150–200 watts, or use 40–60 watts of fluorescent lighting.

Wall lights call for four 50-watt reflector bulbs, or 60–80 watts of fluorescent tubes. *Recessed* units require four 75-watt incandescents or 80 watts of fluorescent lighting.

You'll also need *task lighting.* If you choose a *desk lamp*, the shade's bottom should be 15 inches above the work surface, 15 inches to one side of center, and 12 inches back from the front edge. Use a low-brightness shade with a white lining and a 150-watt soft white bulb for general use or 200 watts for prolonged use.

Fluorescent wall and shelf lights spread light evenly over an entire work area. Locate them 9–12 inches in from the front edge, 15 inches above the work surface, and centered. Select a 36-inch 30-watt, or a 40-inch 40-watt tube.

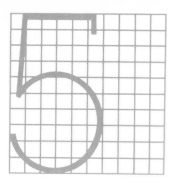

ARTISTS' QUARTERS

If you're in a creative field, where you establish your workplace depends partly on the space available to you and partly on the dictates of your art. Some arts can't be pursued at all without large, specialized equipment, and even the most persistent muse can be thwarted by the lack of an appropriate studio. In other cases, solitude may be as critical to success as the right physical space. In this chapter you'll see eight places where artists hang "Do Not Disturb" signs and get down to business.

THE MUSICIAN

If the tools of your trade are as dazzling as a grand piano and harp, your studio can take center stage. Here, the artist, a performing musician and music teacher, had the living room in this custom-built home designed to double as recital space for her own and her students' performances.

In the bi-level space, the grand piano shares the upper platform with a dining table and eight chairs, visible in the photo *below*. The piano fits into a three-sided bay that projects into the living room. A low glass wall defines the perimeter of the stage without blocking views or sound. Red-carpeted stairways flanking the piano heighten the sense of drama.

A stage lighting system built into a cove above the piano, shown in the photo *opposite*, spotlights the performers. The cove shields globe lights from view, directing the light downward without glaring into the audience's eyes. Recessed downlights in the rest of the ceiling, along with suspended silver globes, create a variety of lighting effects both for performances and for general entertaining.

To keep the performing space as flexible as possible, furniture is held to a minimum. Carpeted benches—one is visible along the pink partial wall in the photo *opposite*—and a couple of armchairs provide the only permanent seating in the room. Additional seating is brought in when needed.

A complete audio system is hidden from view in the partially open closet in the rear of the photo *opposite*.

THE ARTIST

The "ideal" art studio is a place with large, north-facing windows that fill the studio with diffuse, consistent, natural light. But what if such a space isn't available to you? This artist turned his talent toward creating a bright, efficient studio in an unlikely place—a formerly dingy garage and furnace room.

This painter's studio started with paint and canvas. The first step in the transformation was to paint everything in the former garage that could distract the eye. Walls, ceiling, protruding pipes, and storage cabinets were all whited out. Next, the artist stretched and stapled house-painters' drop cloths over the old wooden garage floor. White cloth tape covers the seams in the drop cloths to prevent tripping. Soiled sections can be removed, washed and bleached, then re-stapled in place. The result: a sleek white box that reflects as much light as possible, and

provides a neutral background for displaying paintings.

The garage has a wall with windows (not shown), but they're too small to illuminate the entire work area. The artist built a room-length work counter beneath the windows to take advantage of this natural light. Adjustable track lights brighten the rest of the studio.

The artist often works from photographs, and a large light table pictured *opposite* lets him view transparencies. The table's size lets it double as a desk and conference table.

Back strain is often a problem for artists, who must lean over and reach large work

areas for many hours. This work chair is specially designed to keep the spine in a relaxed, upright position, minimizing fatigue.

In addition to built-in cabinets and closets, this studio is equipped with a low metal cabinet, shown *below,* to organize drawing papers and other materials that need to be stored flat. Art suppliers carry cabinets with drawers of varying depths and widths.

For handy access in any part of the studio, a rolling cart (not shown) stores paints, brushes, and other supplies on top, and stretchers and canvases in vertical slots below.

THE PAINTER/TEACHER

This loft, once occupied by massive printing presses, is now both work space and home to a professional artist and teacher. The urban district in which she lives used to be filled with small factories and warehouses, but hard economic times resulted in many vacancies over the years. This artist and others like her were attracted by the potential in wide-open spaces, high ceilings, and oversize windows.

The ample studio quarters pictured here let the artist fully explore her vision. Her works in progress, several as large as 8x10 feet, line the studio walls. Because her technique involves building up layer upon layer of oil paint, which requires a long drying period, she works on several paintings at the same time.

This 1,000-square-foot studio allows her to develop a whole series of paintings, and work on them in stages. A ladder enables her to reach the tops of the canvases. Storing works as large as these requires a separate room, accessible through the door shown in the background of the photo *below*.

Near the windows, a sturdy 4x8-foot table provides a smooth surface for printmaking and drawing, and offers a convenient place for mixing paints and keeping brushes and other tools close at hand. When life-drawing classes are in session, several students share the table for sketching.

Natural light from the windows is amplified by white walls and a pale gray, glossy-metal ceiling. Hanging globe lights near the beam in the center of the studio can be lowered for working, and tied out of the way close to the ceiling when canvases need to be moved. Long runs of track lighting illuminate the walls.

Tending to business

In one corner of the room, floor-to-ceiling bookshelves and files store reference books, materials, and supply catalogs. An old-fashioned roll-top desk provides a place for corresponding with galleries, arranging showings, and keeping track of sales.

When paintings are ready to be shared with the public, a few quick changes transform this working studio into a gallery. Protective paper is taken up from the floor, supplies are stashed in the storage room, and the worktable becomes a buffet table for serving wine and cheese.

THE PHOTOGRAPHER

A home darkroom needn't always be dark, as the bright, cheerful work space pictured on these pages demonstrates. As long as you devise a means to totally block out light when required, you no longer have to paint the walls of a darkroom black. In fact, the reflectance of a white interior lets you work comfortably with a minimum-wattage safe-light, reducing the possibility of fogging photographic paper. Features that make for an efficient darkroom—access to water, easy-care waterproof surfaces, and plenty of counter space—also come in handy for other pursuits. This darkroom smoothly doubles as a family laundry center, with a washing machine and laundry baskets convenient, yet out of the way, under the counters.

A windowless room is ideal for developing film, but the owner of this darkroom wanted to be able to enjoy a beautiful mountain view when doing laundry or performing photographic tasks that don't require darkness. When she uses the room for developing, she seals the window shown *below* with blackout cloth. (See page 69 for photos and details.)

Weather stripping was installed around the solid wooden door (shown *opposite*) that leads to the rest of the house, to keep light from seeping in around the edges.

This 7x14-foot room allowed for a corridor layout that separates dry and wet processes across the center aisle. Whatever the configuration of your space, you'll need to establish two distinct areas to avoid contaminating negatives and printing papers.

• *Dry* processes don't involve either chemicals or water; they include loading film and paper, enlarging, matting, and mounting. In the darkroom pictured here, an enlarger, a timer, a light box for viewing slides, and file boxes rest on the dry counter. Photographic papers are stored below the counter in extra-wide drawers and shelves. A light-safe drawer that you load with paper prior to printing eliminates fumbling with packages of paper in the dark.

• *Wet* processes, such as developing film and washing prints, use chemicals and water. In the arrangement shown *opposite*, developing trays are set next to each other in sequence of use. Separate tongs for each tray help prevent contamination. A sink large enough to hold your biggest developing tray is ideal for washing prints.

(continued)

In this corridor-style dark-room, a tiled aisle separates dry from wet processes. A lightproof exhaust fan mounted at the end of the wet side pulls moist fumes out; a vent mounted over the dry side brings in fresh air. A laundry facility backs up to the wet side, allowing the darkroom sink to be tied in to existing plumbing.

THE PHOTOGRAPHER

(continued)

Choose a darkroom sink made of a noncorroding material, such as stainless steel, molded plastic, or wood lined with fiberglass, so the chemicals used in processing won't damage it. Building a wood-and-fiberglass sink can be a do-it-yourself project. Photography books provide specific plans and instructions.

• *Water temperature* can be crucial to successful processing, especially if you're developing color film. You can measure water temperature with a thermometer and keep beakers of hot and cold water handy for moderating tray temperatures. A more expensive option is to have the faucet plumbed with a regulator to deliver water at exactly the desired temperature.

• A clothesline or small rack hung over the sink provides a place to clip negatives for drying.

• Try to arrange storage for wet processing materials as near to the sink and developing counter as possible. An efficient arrangement incorporates vertical slot storage for developing trays, and ventilated horizontal trays or screens for drying prints. Cupboards and shelves corral chemicals, beakers, timers, stirrers, sponges, squeegees, and other accessories. If space is tight, consider installing a customized pegboard above the counter to hold supplies.

Safelights

Safelights provide illumination in the darkroom without affecting the light-sensitive papers used for printing. Colors range from several shades of amber to green and red. Instructions provided by the paper manufacturer will tell you what type of safelight (if any) a particular paper can be viewed under. Some safelights come with interchangeable filters so you can vary the color of the light to suit specific papers.

Even the correct lamp can fog paper if the wattage is too high, or if the lamp is too close to the paper. As a rule, select a bulb no stronger than 15 watts, and keep it at least 4 feet above the work surface.

Ventilation and electricity

Sealing out light also means sealing out air, so you'll need to provide ventilation to dispel chemical fumes and bring in fresh air. Photographic supply stores sell lightproof exhaust fans and louvered vents; the best models also feature dust traps that filter incoming air. If possible, install the fan so that it pulls humid air from the wet side of the darkroom directly outside—not past the dry area.

Enlargers, print dryers, lights, and fans can put a strain on wiring. Be sure circuits are properly grounded and have sufficient capacity. Install outlets above your work counters so you can reach them conveniently.

SETTING UP A DARKROOM

The diagram *opposite* illustrates a permanent corridor-style darkroom. Depending on the configuration of your space and the location of the nearest plumbing, a one-wall arrangement with a splash guard erected between wet and dry areas, or an L-shape layout, also will work.

If you don't have space for a complete darkroom, improvise with a temporary setup in a closet, bathroom, or kitchen. In the latter two, you already have water and easy-care surfaces. In a closet darkroom, carry in enough water to fill your developing and holding trays, and wash prints later in another place. You'll need a shelf or counter long enough to accommodate an enlarger and developing trays, separated by a splash guard. Possibilities include a hinged plywood cover that folds down over the tub; a board with folding legs that rests atop the toilet tank and lavatory; and a table set up in the shower. Use a rolling cart to store supplies.

The size of darkroom equipment varies, but below are typical dimensions.

• Enlarger: 14 inches wide by 18 inches deep by 26 inches high (fully extended).
• Dry printer: 18–30 inches wide by 9–14 inches deep by 10–16 inches high.
• Proofing frame: 14 inches by 16 inches.
• Processing trays: 9½ inches by 12 inches (stairstep stacking trays fit into tight quarters).
• Sink: 18 inches by 18 inches by 10 inches deep.
• Counters: 24 inches deep by 5 feet long by 40 inches high.
• Chemical storage: 40 cubic feet.

On the door shown on page 67, a frame of 1x1s with Velcro tacked to its outside edges surrounds the window on the interior side. Matching Velcro strips on the perimeter of the black- **out cloth hold it snugly over the glass. For added protection against strong afternoon sun, another curtain panel snaps onto the outside frame of the entire door.**

THE WEAVER

A hardwood loom strung with colorful yarn is an attractive and intriguing machine, and weaving is a "clean" art. This combination leads many home weavers to set up shop in a family or living room. Professional weavers, however, with one or more large floor looms and bulky stores of yarn, can quickly outgrow family space and require separate studios. This was the case for the weaver whose workplace is pictured here. Built on to the rear of her home, this addition accommodates the diverse needs of this artist, university instructor, and author.

Years of weaving expertise contributed to the efficient design of this studio. Here, the weaver practices, teaches, and writes about her art in a space that smoothly handles all three functions.

Finding the best locations for two massive looms was the first step in organizing the studio. Large south and west windows bring in lots of daylight, and the looms were oriented to take advantage of the natural light without being directly in its path. Direct sun shining onto the looms can cause the weaving to fade unevenly and

distort its colors. Track lighting and recessed fixtures under the balcony pictured *opposite* provide additional light when needed. (Fluorescent lighting is not recommended for weaving studios because it tends to fade fabrics faster than incandescent sources.) Because the weight of the looms fixes their locations in the studio, storage was planned around them. Closets with folding wooden doors protect stores of yarn from dust and light. Bobbins and other supplies for the works currently in progress rest on recessed open shelves within easy reach of the looms.

Spreaders, shuttles, niddy noddies, and other tools move from one loom to the other in open roll-around containers, one of which is shown in the photo *below*. The weaver sits on a loom bench with a slightly slanted top that allows her to lean into the loom as she works.

Easily swept ceramic mosaic tile—laid over a concrete slab base—adds subtle pattern to the large expanse of floor space. Any smooth surface, such as resilient flooring or even painted concrete, would work equally well.

(continued)

THE WEAVER
(continued)

One wall of the studio pictured *at right* is devoted to the academic facet of this weaver's career. Reference books fill a double tier of built-in shelves over a desk. Floor-to-ceiling cabinets house more supplies and teaching materials.

Planning your own studio

The drawing *opposite* illustrates features you should take into account when designing your studio. You'll want an arrangement that lets you maneuver easily around the loom and store supplies close at hand. A planning table is a useful extra. If you're tight on space, consider a hinged unit that folds out of the way when it's not in use.

How much space you need for weaving depends largely on the type of loom you select. Beginners might start with a portable table loom, but serious weavers usually move on to floor looms, which allow them to weave larger fabrics with more complicated patterns.

Looms are sized according to the maximum width of the fabric web you can produce on them. You can weave materials from 20 to 60 inches wide, with table looms handling a maximum width of 32 inches. Experienced weavers recommend buying the widest width you can afford and house, because you can weave narrow pieces on a wide loom, but not the reverse.

With a table loom, all work is done with the hands; with floor models, treadles attached to the harnesses let you use your feet to shift the shed.

Floor looms are either *counterbalance* or *jack* type. With a counterbalance loom, the harnesses operate in pairs; with a jack loom, each harness moves independently.

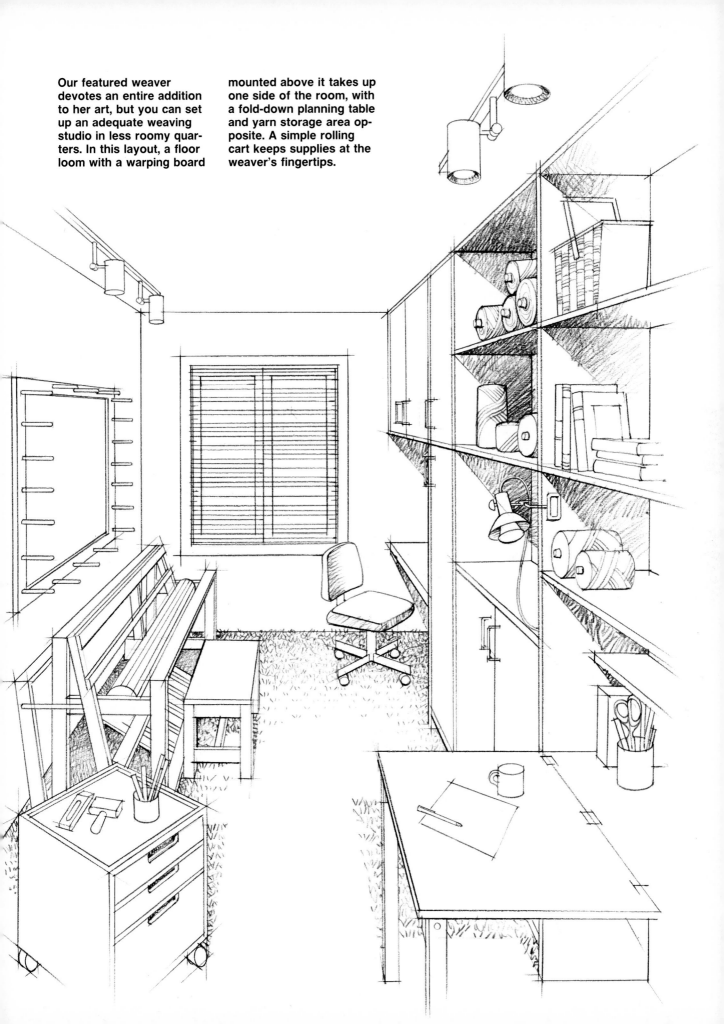

Our featured weaver devotes an entire addition to her art, but you can set up an adequate weaving studio in less roomy quarters. In this layout, a floor loom with a warping board mounted above it takes up one side of the room, with a fold-down planning table and yarn storage area opposite. A simple rolling cart keeps supplies at the weaver's fingertips.

THE POTTER

If you've grown to love plunging your hands into cool, wet clay and letting your imagination take shape, you may be ready for your own home studio. The shed-roof structure pictured on these pages is one potter's custom-crafted workplace. Connected by a wooden walkway to the main house, this studio provides a private place for the owner to pursue her art, and plenty of room for students. Low-slung double-glazed windows direct light where the potter needs it most, and act as solar collectors in the winter. In summer, when the sun travels in a higher arc, the studio remains pleasantly cool. Cool temperatures are especially important for keeping stored clay moist. Equipped with a small kitchen and bathroom, the studio provides a retreat for times when the artist seeks solitude. A sleeping loft above the work area lets the studio double as a guesthouse.

Whether your studio is as ambitious as the one pictured here, or more modest quarters in a basement or garage, you'll need to plan for certain essentials.

• Install rugged, easy-to-clean floor surfaces that take spatters in stride, such as concrete, resilients, or tile.

• For convenient access to water, try to locate your studio near existing plumbing. A deep sink such as the one pictured *opposite,* fitted with a silt-collecting trap, is ideal.

• A large, sturdy worktable is a must. The one shown *opposite* is made of 2x4s on edge joined with threaded rods.

• To prepare raw clay, set up a *wedging* surface—a slab of plaster or wood on part of the main worktable or on its own sturdy base.

• Tight-fitting garbage cans lined with heavy-duty plastic bags make good containers for bulk clay.

• Locate your *potter's wheel* where you can take advantage of natural light. You can choose one operated by a foot-powered kick wheel or a more expensive electric one.

• A *banding wheel,* a hand-operated turntable used for making coiled pots, also lets you turn a project for finishing and applying glazes.

• *Shelves* and more shelves. They'll quickly fill up with glazes and works in progress.

• Your largest investment will be a *kiln.* Small portable electric models run on standard household current; larger electric kilns require 240-volt lines. You'll need to provide a flue for a gas-fired unit. If the floor beneath the kiln is made of flammable material, protect it with a layer of fire brick. (More about setting up a pottery studio on pages 80 and 81.)

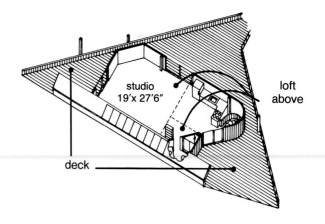

studio
19'x 27'6"

loft
above

deck

THE QUILTER

This craftswoman's studio is as warm and welcoming as the quilts she designs and sews. A home away from home, her studio, along with her husband's, is housed in a separate barnlike building on their farm property. A downstairs showroom takes up the ground floor, and a shared area between the two studios includes office space, storage for books, slides, and promotional materials, and a mini-kitchen that minimizes trips back and forth to the main house.

This artist's vibrant, graphic quilts are hand-made from start to finish. She weaves and dyes her own fabrics, strips of which hang from a convenient wooden rack beside the sewing machine, shown in the photo *opposite*. In front of the windows, an oak table provides a large, smooth surface for cutting fabrics and laying out patterns. A multidrawer, wall-hung cabinet organizes notions.

The ironing board is kept close at hand, yet out of the way, in a built-in cabinet under the stairs.

Modeled after a 150-year-old barn that once stood on the site, the studio boasts 14½-foot-high ceilings that accommodate a loft above the main work area. Here, under a pair of skylights, the artist works out new quilt designs at a drawing board. The loft also doubles as a guest bedroom.

On the side of the room opposite the loft (out of camera range), she set up her loom beneath three large windows. Plank flooring gives a warm glow to the whole space, and is a practical surface as well. Bits of thread and fabric that

would become embedded in carpeting are easily swept off the smooth surface.

Adding a detached year-round work area meant heating another building in addition to the house. This studio uses passive solar principles to keep energy costs down. Floor-to-ceiling windows in the south wall of the downstairs showroom let in sunlight, which is captured in a brick floor. Upstairs, large south-facing windows let in both heat and natural light. A ceiling fan in the peak of the roof helps circulate air.

A FAMILY OF ARTISTS

Art is often thought of as a solitary pursuit, and many artists do prefer to work alone. Others, however, enjoy having company. When art is a family affair, a shared studio can be both a productive workplace and a congenial gathering place. Provided with their own scaled-down equipment, children can work side by side with their parents. And with children busily engaged and within view, parents can accomplish a lot, too.

This skylighted studio is the creation of an architect who wanted a place at home to finish architectural drawings, build models of his plans, and pursue hobbies. Away from his family during business hours, he wanted a home studio where his wife and young daughter could join him. A weekend afternoon might find him sketching at his drawing board, his wife working on a stained-glass project, and their daughter painting at her own child-size easel.

Their U-shape work station is made of three equal-size modular desks, all with plastic laminate surfaces. The top of one module, pictured *opposite,* can be raised from a standard flat desktop to a slanted drawing board. The arrangement provides each person with individual work and storage space.

A convenient configuration for two, a U-shape setup also is handy for a single person at work on more than one project. When work needs demand it, the desks can be rearranged easily.

Built-in bookcases surrounding a window in the background house the family's art books and magazines for ready reference. Unadorned windows let in plenty of light and offer hilltop vistas of a valley below the house. At night, sliding shutter panels close off the windows to conserve energy.

As the floor plans illustrate, space for the studio was garnered from two former bedrooms. Opening the ceiling to the roofline created room for an upstairs loft that recovers some of the lost sleeping space. A skylight brightens the soaring half of the studio, and a fir-clad dropped ceiling creates a cozy section below the loft.

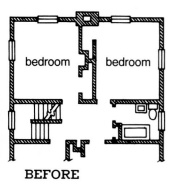

bedroom   bedroom

BEFORE

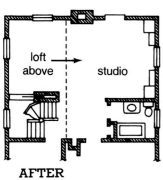

loft
above   studio

AFTER

PLANNING ARTISTS' QUARTERS

As you've seen on the preceding pages, artists' quarters are as varied as the artists themselves. Some pursuits require bulky, specialized equipment and a permanent setup; other arts can comfortably share space with daily family activities. We've illustrated a layout for a potter's work space, *at right,* because this craft demands much equipment, access to water, and, often, electrical circuits that can carry more than standard household current. You can include or adapt many features of this studio in your own work center.

First, decide *where* to locate your studio. If running water is necessary, can you combine quarters with the kitchen, a bathroom, or the laundry room? For arts that need independent spaces, the closer you are to an existing wet wall, the lower the plumbing costs for the new facility.

How will you bring in supplies and how much do they weigh? Potters often prefer ground-level studios because bags of raw clay are heavy. A converted garage that you can drive right into with supplies can be an ideal spot. Consider, too, that heavy equipment, such as a large kiln, may need an extra-strong floor to support it.

Most artists prefer to work under natural light as much as possible. If the space you have in mind has few or small windows, consider enlarging the openings, or adding new windows or skylights. Our illustration supplements window light with a luminous ceiling. In this type of installation, fluorescent tubes, or, less frequently, incandescent lamps, are concealed behind translucent panels or louvered grids to provide even, glare-free illumination.

If accurate color perception is vital, select color-corrected fluorescents, which closely approximate northern daylight. For a cozier environment, you may prefer warm-tone fluorescent or incandescent sources.

A breath of fresh air can spur creativity, and adequate ventilation is essential if your art involves toxic chemicals or extreme heat. Locate heat-generating equipment, such as a kiln, as far from your general work area as possible. Install an exhaust fan through a wall or in a window to quickly dissipate heat, moisture, or fumes.

NUMBERS TO KNOW

Table easels will support a stretched canvas 15 to 22 inches high.

Adjustable floor easels extend to heights of about 66 to 100 inches.

Drawing tables come in board sizes of 23x31 to 37½x72 inches.

Drafting tables feature board sizes of 37x60 to 43x84 inches.

Plan files with large flat drawers come in a variety of depths, and widths up to 50 inches.

Kilns that run on household current feature firing chambers with openings of 6½ to 15 inches, depths of 6½ to 15½ inches, and cubic-foot capacities of .16 to 1.7. Models that require 240-volt lines have openings of 11 to 36 inches, depths of 11 to 45 inches, and cubic-foot capacities of .77 to 27. Gas kilns for home use range in capacity from 3.95 to 20 cubic feet.

This potter's studio is located in a converted garage, whose large front door can be opened to provide ventilation and natural light in warm weather. Bulky bags of raw clay can be driven in and conveniently unloaded and stored. The concrete floor washes clean with a hose, and is strong enough, without structural modification, to support the weight of the kiln.

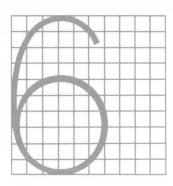

SHOPS

Do you find yourself tinkering with broken appliances on the kitchen counter, just because you lack a convenient place for household repairs? Has a small collection of tools grown by a few wrenches here and a drill and saber saw there into an unwieldy assortment? Or perhaps you're hooked on the beauty of wood and want to be able to build your own shelves, cabinets, or furniture, or create handcrafts that beg to be touched. If you recognize yourself in any of these descriptions, it's time to set up an organized home workshop.

To own a home is to inevitably face an assortment of odd jobs, routine repairs, and improvement projects. There's always a door that sticks, a curtain rod to install, a kit to assemble. For some tasks all you really need is a toolbox with a selection of basic hand tools. Other jobs go more smoothly when you have a work surface to spread out on and a permanent home for a larger collection of more specialized tools and supplies.

As long as your puttering place is planned on a fairly small scale, it usually won't require an entire room. Look for an area that's outside the mainstream of family activity and provides enough space for you to store tools and supplies and leave unfinished projects between work sessions. Attics, basements, spare bedrooms, family rooms, and especially garages are all viable candidates for puttering places. Garages rate high on the list because they offer ground-level access, and large doors for moving projects and supplies in and out of the shop.

A shop down under
The work station shown *opposite* is an example of how an efficient shop can comfortably share a basement room with other facilities. The homeowners staked out one corner of a utility room for their workbench and tools; the furnace and laundry machines occupy other parts of the room.

Bright ceiling tiles, new fluorescent lights, and a vinyl floor dramatically changed the appearance of the previously unfinished basement. The smooth resilient floor makes a quick sweep of any messes, and provides much more comfort underfoot than the old concrete floor did. A sturdy

workbench wraps around a corner and has plenty of storage room on and below shelves. Perforated hardboard mounted above the workbench organizes tools in plain sight.

Getting organized
One need for every workshop, large or small, is organization. It usually takes longer to find a tool not returned to its proper spot than it would have taken to return it in the first place. Keep frequently used tools right at your fingertips. If you need shelf space, consider building or buying shallow shelves that keep most objects visible. Stack wood in several neat piles rather than in one jumbled heap.

Good lighting is essential for safety when using tools. Besides, you'll be more satisfied with the results if you work under light as bright as or brighter than the light the finished work will be viewed under.

Be sure to provide adequate ventilation so you don't breathe in sawdust or the vapors from chemicals, paints, and adhesives. If air doesn't circulate, install an exhaust fan and/or new windows and doors.

If you're especially tight on space, you can get by with less than a formal workshop. Some families manage all their projects out of a toolbox, supplemented by perforated hardboard storage mounted on a closet wall or on the back of a door. Collapsible, portable workbenches have become popular space savers with weekend handymen and professional woodworkers alike.

A GARAGE
WORKSHOP

The owner of the efficient workshop pictured here had been laboring "out back" for years in a dilapidated garage built in 1910. After worrying about the unstable structure and antiquated wiring, he decided to raze the garage and rebuild from scratch. The new 12x24-foot building serves several needs, housing a garage and garden and tool storage area as well as a shop. In addition, a loft over the shop provides work space for his wife, a weaver.

The owners of this garage/shop contracted an architect to design and build the shell of the structure, but decided to complete the interior themselves. That way, they not only saved money, but also were able to tailor it to their own specifications.

Separating each use was a top priority. One outside door opens directly to the garden storage area so the lawn mower and other yard tools don't have to be dragged through the workshop and garage. An outside flight of stairs leads to the weaving loft above the workshop. Off to one side of the shop area, bikes are parked beneath elevated cabinets in which infrequently used paints are stored.

The design of this garage workshop encourages frequent use. Many projects can be accomplished while a car is parked in the garage. Or for work that needs a lot of space, the entire garage can be commandeered.

Attention to detail

The same meticulous craftsmanship the homeowner puts into his cabinet work is evident in the design of the shop storage facilities. In the photo *at right,* you can see that careful planning went into perforated hardboard tool storage units. Before the walls were covered, see-through drawer units for hardware were set between studs to take advantage of dead space.

Years of woodworking expertise led to the design of the workbench and its immediate surroundings pictured

opposite. An overhang around the countertop makes it easy to clamp wood securely to the bench. For additional rigidity, the back edge of the counter is fastened to the wall. Three shelves beneath the workbench help organize lumber into manageable stacks. Behind the wood collage (one example of the homeowner's handiwork) propped up in the lower left-hand corner is another cabinet for storing lumber. Out of camera range, a lockable floor-to-ceiling cabinet keeps supplies and frequently used hand and electrical tools organized, dust-free, and safe from curious children.

A rollaway tool-storage cabinet next to the bicycle matches the 35-inch height of the workbench. The woodworker can

roll this unit anywhere and use both surfaces to support long boards or large projects.

Even the window frame does its share of tool storage. Holes drilled into the ledge provide an ideal space to stick screwdrivers and nail sets. The window ledge itself acts as a buffer so wood on the workbench can be butted up against it. Frequently used measuring and marking tools hang above the window.

This woodworker found a way to take advantage of the belt clips on his tape measures. He attached 1x3-inch metal plates over depressions routed into the inside stop of the window. Now the tape measures slide onto the metal "belt" and hang highly visible and within easy reach.

A WORKSHOP ADDITION

After nine years in a 9x13-foot basement workshop, one home furniture maker put his talents to work by designing and building a ground-level workshop that more than tripled his floor space. Keeping resale of the home in mind, he finished the 16x24-foot addition with tongue-and-groove cedar strips so it could be easily converted to a family room by a future owner.

Woodworking in such stylish surroundings encouraged this craftsman to conquer two nagging shop problems: organization and dust control.

All of his hand and power tools are kept where they are most apt to be used *and* returned to their proper places. As you can see in the large photo and lower inset *opposite,* extensive use of white perforated hardboard keeps many tools, clamps, and accessories right at the woodworker's fingertips, and also reflects additional light around the room.

Sawdust isn't given an opportunity to linger in this shop. Every major power tool can be connected to one of two canister vacuum cleaners. Dust and wood chips from the table saw and the jointer in the foreground of the photo *below* can be sucked up while both machines are running; a T-fitting of PVC plastic facilitates this operation. The owner also designed a dust catcher on the radial-arm saw, shown in the upper inset *opposite*, to deflect sawdust into a hole where it, too, is sucked up by a vacuum. The 25-degree angle of the catcher and the shield behind the saw eliminates most of the sawdust.

If, despite the collectors, sawdust still gets out of hand, two exhaust fans mounted in the window clear the air.

Double doors shown in the photo *opposite* provide a wide opening that alleviates the gymnastics the owner used to go through to bring 4x8-foot sheets of plywood into his former workshop. Once he has them inside, a custom-designed wood caddy serves as a "third hand" to help maneuver the plywood sheets for cutting. Visible in the lower left-hand portion of the photo *below,* this rolling-pin-topped caddy supports and feeds wood toward the saw.

Additional features in this shop include sound-deadening materials in the walls and ceilings, retractable ceiling-mounted extension cords, and a concealed forced-air furnace.

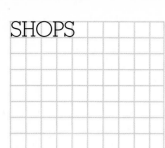

A CRAFTS ROOM

Although this hobbyist's craft uses wood, it doesn't require a full-scale woodworking shop like the ones pictured on the previous pages. A jigsaw and drill are the only power tools needed to turn out hand-painted wooden puzzles and toys. Because this craft is relatively quiet and neat, the hobby shop and a home office coexist comfortably.

Here's proof that even a diminutive bedroom can serve as a shop—provided that the making of your projects doesn't take up a lot of space and isn't overly noisy or messy. In this former spare room, a puzzle- and toy-maker has pieced together three separate work stations: one for woodworking, another for paperwork, and a third for thinking out the details of a project.

The key to the division is a long peninsula in the middle of the room, visible in the foreground of the photo *at right*. It provides a surface for spreading out and painting projects. Nearby, a jigsaw sits on a metal cart that can be rolled to any part of this well-lit room. When not in use, the saw pushes back against the wall between a pair of storage units.

A large work surface surrounds the jigsaw, making it easier to cut out puzzles and other detail work. Plywood panels flip up on each side of the jigsaw for access to additional storage space.

What once was a built-in closet now serves as an office and design area. After the sliding closet doors were removed, shelves, a plastic-laminate work surface, and a two-drawer file cabinet were added.

On the shelves, crafts books and storage bins for small supplies sit close at hand. Crafts catalogs, patterns, clipped

ideas, and other reference materials are neatly organized in the file cabinet. An adjustable office chair offers comfortable seating.

Additional supplies can be stored in a smaller closet to the right of the design area, as shown in the floor plan *below*. Here, lazy Susans on the shelves help keep supplies organized.

Shelves spanning the windows attractively display other materials in clear containers. Larger tools and supplies hang on perforated hardboard attached to one wall. A drying rack joins the peninsula counter to the wall and makes a handy place to air rags and towels.

Because thinking about projects also is important, an armchair in front of a window makes an excellent retreat to relax and read. A bookshelf helps screen the corner from the rest of the room.

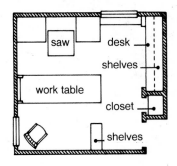

SETTING UP
A HOME WORKSHOP

Although no one serves meals from a workbench, there are many similarities between a kitchen and a workshop. If well-designed and adequately equipped, both places can be efficient, pleasurable environments for creative work. In a workshop, as in a kitchen, you have to make optimum use of space. Often the room's shape isn't ideal, and its proportions may seem cramped, but a good shop isn't necessarily a big shop.

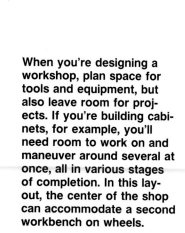

When you're designing a workshop, plan space for tools and equipment, but also leave room for projects. If you're building cabinets, for example, you'll need room to work on and maneuver around several at once, all in various stages of completion. In this layout, the center of the shop can accommodate a second workbench on wheels.

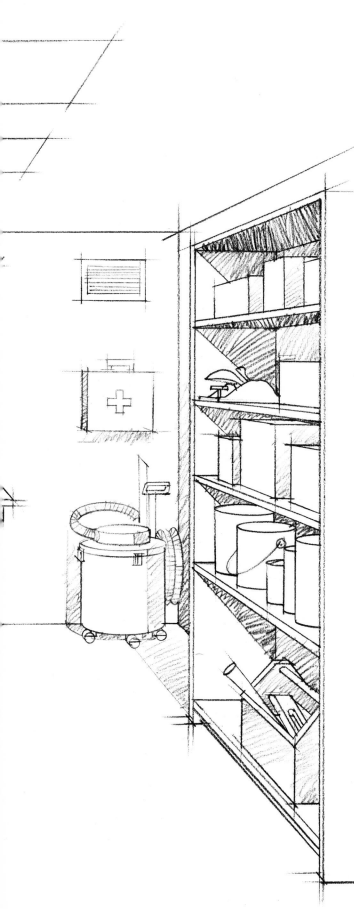

Wherever you decide to set up your workshop, follow these guidelines to make it useful and efficient:

• *Design.* Because most shop work takes place at a bench, this is the logical focus of any shop. Remember that work triangle so important in kitchen design? It's just as important in any shop—and especially well used in the one illustrated *at left*. The workbench is one point of the triangle; a cabinet filled with portable power tools at the far left serves as the second point; at the right, supplies and hand tools on open shelves occupy the third point.

Remember to keep your arrangement flexible enough to absorb additional tools and bulky projects. A workbench on wheels or a fold-down work bench would be a useful addition to this or any other shop because it allows for work on all sides of a project.

• *Safety.* Carelessly used and poorly maintained, tools can inflict a lot of damage, so keep cutting edges sharp and everything in good repair.

A shop should have at least one 20-amp electrical circuit; consider having it professionally wired with a ground-fault circuit interrupter (GFCI) for additional shock protection. For shadowless illumination that won't dim when you turn on a heavy-duty motor, wire lights on a separate circuit. Install a fan to vent fumes and sawdust, and keep a fire extinguisher and first aid kit in an easily reached location.

If there are children in your home, keep dangerous tools and poisonous materials locked or far out of their reach. Unplug power tools before leaving your workshop and install a lock on the door to keep out curious children. Some stationary power tools

are keyed or sold with accessory locks for an added measure of safety.

• *Comfort.* Work surfaces should suit your size. Save your back and build the workbench and sawhorses to suit your height, as explained on pages 92 and 93. Take care of your feet, too. Instead of standing on an unyielding concrete basement floor, as many woodworkers do, place a rubber pad in front of the workbench. And while you're thinking about comfort, take into consideration the comfort of other family members and neighbors. Does your workshop need sound-deadening material?

• *Organization and visibility.* It's much easier to find things if you can see them. Perforated hardboard installed on walls provides an excellent way to organize hand tools. Shallow shelves, such as those to the right of the workbench, are ideal for keeping track of supplies, paints, and additional tools. Drawer units such as the one on the workbench keep hardware organized and at your fingertips. Some woodworkers use baby food jars and other inexpensive containers to store items. Consider storing smaller pieces of wood overhead between floor joists.

• *Cleanup.* As it is in the kitchen, cleaning up is an inevitable chore in a shop. Attack sawdust with a shop vacuum and also reserve a broom, bench brush, dustpan, and trash can for exclusive use in your workshop. Rags soaked with flammables should be stored in covered metal cans or outside the house.

BUILDING BENCHES AND SAWHORSES

Good workbenches quietly take all the pushing, pounding, clamping, and sawing you can dish out. You can invest hundreds of dollars in a fancy European-designed workbench with several vises, bench dogs to hold odd-shaped projects, and unique hold-down clamps. Or you can plan and build your own bench, save a lot of money, and have a reliable workshop partner designed for you, your shop, and the type of woodworking you do. The same goes for sawhorses and toolboxes, which you can purchase ready-made or construct by adapting the designs shown here.

A BASIC WORKBENCH

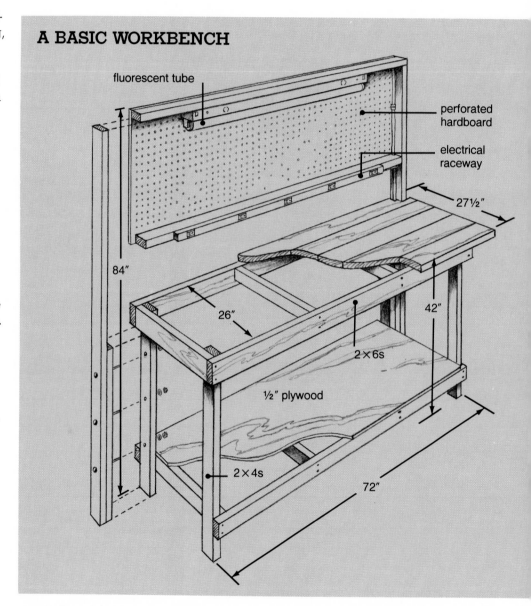

fluorescent tube

perforated hardboard

electrical raceway

84"

27½"

26"

42"

2 × 6s

½" plywood

2 × 4s

72"

Sturdiness is the key to a successful workbench. The one illustrated *above* is supported by pine 2x4s and has a top made of pine 2x6s. You also can laminate two ¾-inch sheets of plywood and then nail or screw tempered hardboard to the top for a smooth surface that can be easily replaced. This project may be assembled with glue and nails; for more rigidity, use lag screws instead of nails.

Most woodworkers are comfortable with a workbench counter that's equal in height to the top of their hips. If you plan to assemble a lot of cabinets, make one counter several inches lower.

If you prefer to use a bench in the middle of your workshop, eliminate the perforated hardboard back and electrical raceway shown here and use a retractable extension cord installed overhead.

The versatile rollaway workbench detailed *above right* is a great problem solver. Where space is at a premium, it can be tucked beneath shelves in a closet, as shown. In a more spacious shop, it could be rolled to the middle of the

A ROLLAWAY WORKBENCH

measurements
vary with
closet depth
and width

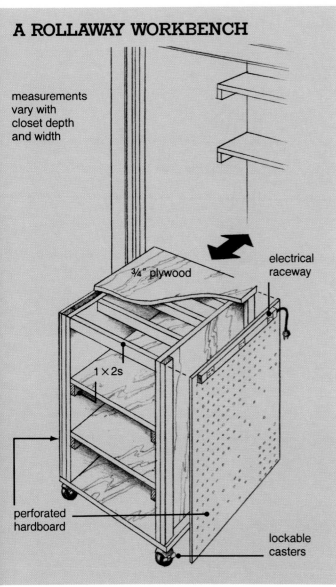

electrical
raceway

¾" plywood

1 × 2s

perforated
hardboard

lockable
casters

SAWHORSE BASICS

¾" plywood
gusset

2 × 6s

1 × 4

30"

24"

42"

metal
brackets

hinged
metal legs

TOOLBOX BASICS

1¼" dowel

16"

1 × 3s

12"

30"

room where you can work from all sides.

Sawhorses are indispensable for cutting long stock or plywood sheets and for use as temporary work surfaces for large, bulky projects. Build a pair from scratch, like the larger one shown *at upper right*, or assemble them from hardware store components, as the ones below it were. One de-sign includes a set of brackets into which you insert five lengths of 2x4; the other uses hinged metal legs and requires only one 2x4.

Home center stores offer a wide variety of metal toolboxes, some so capacious that they have wheels underneath. Or build your own open, two-tray carrier according to our specifications.

CHOOSING AND USING HAND TOOLS

BASIC HAND TOOLS

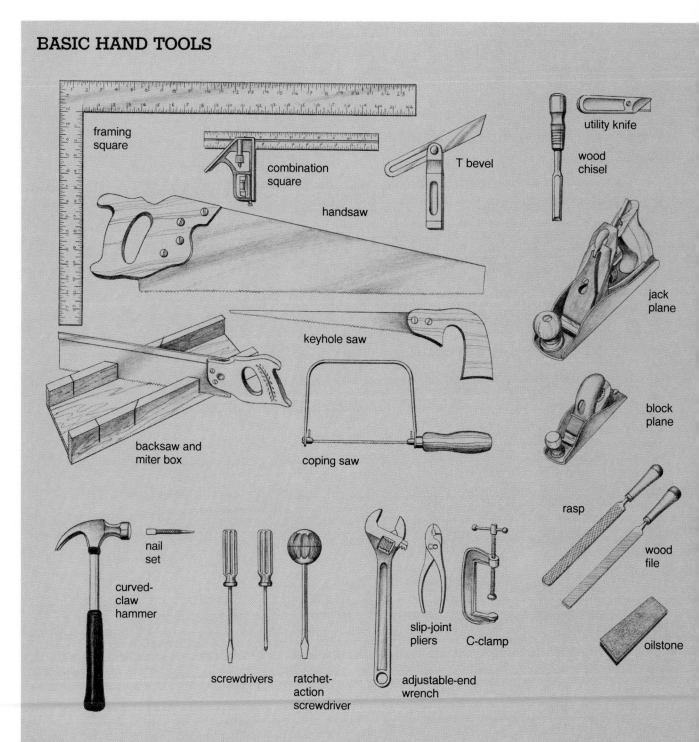

framing square

combination square

T bevel

utility knife

wood chisel

handsaw

jack plane

keyhole saw

backsaw and miter box

coping saw

block plane

rasp

nail set

curved-claw hammer

screwdrivers

ratchet-action screwdriver

slip-joint pliers

C-clamp

adjustable-end wrench

wood file

oilstone

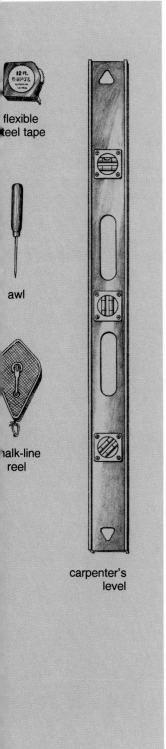

flexible
steel tape

awl

chalk-line
reel

carpenter's
level

Working with inferior tools often leads to inferior workmanship and frustration. Tools aren't meant to be disposable; the tools you buy should be of the highest quality you can afford, and the one tool you can't afford to buy is the bargain tool. Consider middle-quality tools, often called the consumer line, or a manufacturer's professional line of tools. Several companies stand behind their best line with a lifetime guarantee: If a tool breaks or becomes unusable, it will be replaced. Think of high-quality tools as an investment in work made easy.

If you're setting up your first shop, or find yourself struggling with jobs in your present shop because you lack the right tools, check the following inventory. These hand tools form the core of a workshop; add others as needs arise.

Measuring and marking tools
You probably own a *flexible steel tape*. Twelve to 25 feet of tape are wound into a compact case. Better models retract automatically and feature a lock button. The *framing square* checks right angles and stud spacing and also can be used to mark stair and rafter cuts. The *combination square* checks right- and 45-degree angles and can be used as a depth gauge. Many models include a small spirit level and a scratch awl. A 24- or 28-inch *carpenter's level* is the standard spirit level. It can be used to check large projects for level or plumb. The *T-bevel* can duplicate angles up to 180 degrees. Use an *awl* to mark cut lines and to make pilot holes.

Hammers. The 16-ounce *curved claw hammer* you depend upon for general carpentry should have a secure head and a comfortable handle. To sink finish nail heads below the surface, you'll need at least one *nail set*.

Screwdrivers. You need to have several sizes of standard and Phillips (X-slot) screwdrivers. By changing the direction of a thumb slide, a *ratchet-action screwdriver* can drive or back out screws.

Saws. If you plan to own only one *handsaw*, make a 26-inch *crosscut saw* your choice. This saw can cut with and across the wood grain. A *keyhole saw* has a narrow blade for cutting in tight areas and for negotiat-

ing curves. The *coping saw* can make intricate curves in thin stock. The *back saw* in a *miter box* makes accurate, smooth angle cuts. Also consider adding a *hacksaw* for cutting metal and plastic.

Chisels. *Wood chisels* often are sold in sets of three to five chisels in varying widths. The more expensive chisels have higher quality steel that holds an edge longer. Select chisels with a comfortable, metal-capped handle.

Planes. A *jack plane* can be used to plane edge joints and smooth wide surfaces. The low angle of the blade in the *block plane* is excellent for planing end grain and small pieces.

Clamps. *C-clamps* are necessary for holding pieces together while glue dries. For holding framework or wider boards together, consider buying *pipe* or *T-bar clamps*.

Pliers. In addition to grabbing small objects, *slip-joint pliers* can be used to cut wire. Channel-type pliers handle work too large for slip-joint pliers.

Wrenches. One or more adjustable open-end *wrenches* find their way into most tool chests. Also popular are fixed-end wrenches and socket sets.

Files and rasps. The bastard double-cut *wood file* is the most popular for smoothing wood. *Rasps* are coarser than files and quickly remove a lot of wood. Also consider a surface-shaping tool with a replaceable, rasplike blade.

Miscellaneous. A *utility knife* is handy for doing light cutting. Use a *chalk line* to snap a long straight line; most chalk-line boxes also can be used as plumb bobs to mark vertical lines. An *oilstone* is necessary to keep a sharp edge on chisels and plane irons. Some stones are coarse on one side, with a harder stone on the other for a fine finish.

CHOOSING AND USING POWER TOOLS

Not so long ago, all tools were hand tools, and you can still complete many projects without power tools. Most woodworkers, however, want to take advantage of the speed, accuracy, and ease that electricity has brought to the workshop. You'll probably want to start with a few versatile and affordable portable power tools. Stationary power tools are a big investment, but a natural progression for a person developing a keener interest in woodworking.

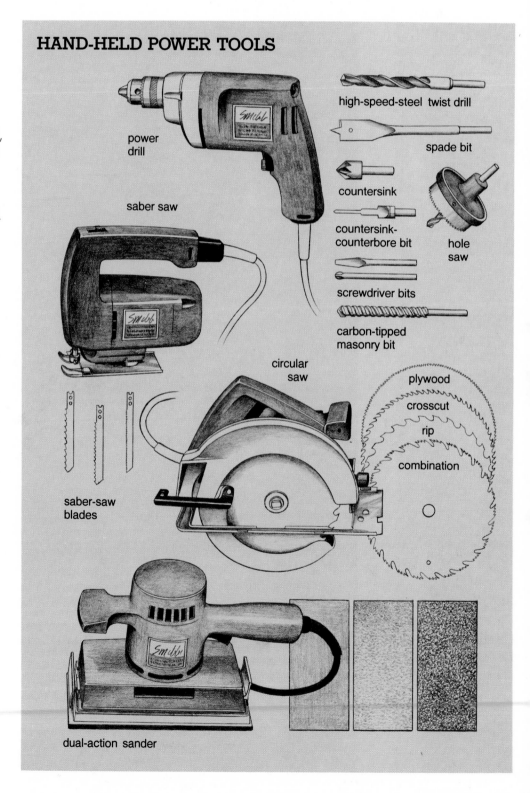

HAND-HELD POWER TOOLS

power drill

saber saw

high-speed-steel twist drill

spade bit

countersink

countersink-counterbore bit

hole saw

screwdriver bits

carbon-tipped masonry bit

circular saw

saber-saw blades

plywood

crosscut

rip

combination

dual-action sander

Hand-held power tools have one great advantage over stationary tools: You take the tool to the job, not the other way around.

Power drills are rated by the maximum diameter of bit shafts the chuck can accept; most have a chuck capacity of ¼, ⅜, or ½ inch. The ⅜-inch drill is the most popular for home use because it has enough power to handle most jobs, yet is not as heavy to hold as the ½-inch drill. Select a drill that has a variable-speed trigger and a reverse switch; these features are especially important if you plan to use your drill as a power screwdriver.

If you're shopping for a portable *circular saw,* you'll get a lot of service from a 7¼-inch model with a 1¼-horsepower motor; this saw can easily buzz through 2-inch-thick boards and most plywood. A hand-held circular saw is especially handy for cutting large sheets of plywood into sizes that can be more easily maneuvered to a table or radial-arm saw. Important features are: an automatic blade guard, tilt mechanism, rip fence accessory, and a saw blade depth adjustment.

A *saber saw* can't make straight cuts as accurately as a circular saw can, but it remains a versatile power tool. Its major selling point is its ability to cut curves in all types of materials, including wood, metal, and plastic. Solid construction and power are the most important considerations; the saber saw should be able to cut through 2-inch-thick material without the blade wandering. Fence and circle-cutting attachments are practical and affordable.

Dual-action sanders perform two different motions. In the orbital mode, rough surfaces are quickly removed. When the sander is switched to a straight-line action, this tool becomes a finish sander.

Stationary power tools

Which will it be: a table saw or a radial-arm saw? Each has its strengths.

The *table saw* makes fast and accurate rips and crosscuts and is the preferred saw for cutting sheet goods such as 4x8-foot panels. A saw with an 8- to 10-inch blade and a ¾- to 1-horsepower motor is suitable for most home uses. Most of the blade is below the cutting surface; to use the saw, you push the wood into the blade. Entire books about cutting jigs for the table saw have been written by innovative craftsmen.

The *radial-arm saw* also is versatile; most agree it beats the table saw at crosscutting. All of the blade is above the work so it is easier to see the cut as it is being made. For crosscuts, you hold the wood stationary and pull the blade through it. Accessories for the radial-arm saw make it possible for it to be used for planing and sanding.

Keep your hand tools sharp by acquiring a *bench grinder.* A ¼- to ½-horsepower motor with grinding guides is a considerably smaller investment than either of the tools discussed above.

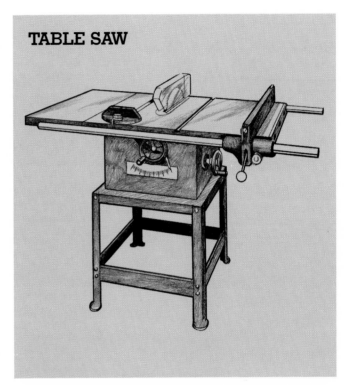

TABLE SAW

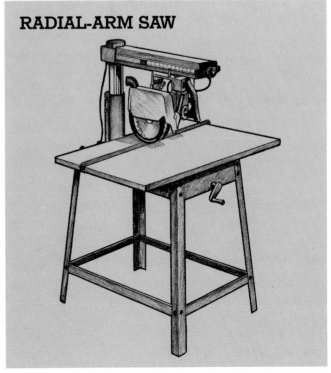

RADIAL-ARM SAW

bench grinder

97

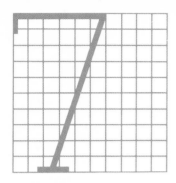

HOME BUSINESS BASICS

One day, you're just a talented amateur, pursuing your interest. The next, you're expected to be a home-based professional, savvy and sophisticated in the ways of small business. Is the transition possible? With preparation, yes. Everyone who plans to work at home should devote some time to learning the basics of business, from financial and legal matters to record keeping and taxes. Whether you're a hobbyist turning pro or someone trading a traditional office spot for a desk at home, being businesslike is a key to your success. Ultimately, it's what separates the marginal performers from the money-makers.

You're eager to start your home venture, but perhaps you feel a bit overwhelmed by the business aspects. Relax! When you take things step by logical step and seek the help of experts, the challenges seem less awesome.

If you've decided on the nature of your business and its home location, two of your toughest decisions are already behind you. Now, you enter an important stage of gathering facts, doing informal market research, and setting goals.

You'll eventually synthesize all this in the form of a business plan. Every business, regardless of size or type, needs this important written document. Formats will vary, but all plans should address certain basic questions: What is the purpose of my business? Who will buy my product or service, and for how much? What is my competition? How will I attract customers? How much money will I need to start and run my business?

Many good sources of help are available as you seek the answers you need.

• *Small Business Administration (SBA).* This federal agency's purpose is to provide information and guidance to America's small business owners. Visit a field office, if possible. Ask about counseling services and seminars, and review the SBA's comprehensive list of free or low-cost publications.

• *Industry associations.* These groups regularly survey their members on prices, marketing trends, and other issues. Their published statistics, newsletters, and directories can offer valuable insight into your field. If you're not sure whether your industry has an association, check the Encyclopedia of Associations in the public library.

• *Financial institutions.* Banks and thrift institutions want new businesses to succeed, so many offer counseling and financial planning services.

• *Accounting firms.* The major accounting firms, particularly those known as the "Big Eight," are trying to win small-business clients; they publish useful booklets about various aspects of starting and running a business.

• *Personal contacts.* Talk to others who do what you want to do. Find them through professional associations, or check the Yellow Pages for small business owners in your field. If those in your area are hesitant to talk, try others out of competitive range.

Making plans
Now you're ready to draft a preliminary plan. Having your thoughts organized will make it easier to talk with the experts you'll need to consult. A lawyer can help you settle on the best legal form of business for your situation—see the chart on page 99 for some advantages and disadvantages of each—and draw up necessary forms. An accountant can show you an effective way to keep your books and counsel you on your tax obligations. A banker can look at your financial picture, and give advice about borrowing and loans. And the insurance broker will explain the types of coverage you need, and make sure you're well-protected against peril.

One hint during these preliminary steps: Don't worry about having your own business forms printed at this stage. Large stationery stores carry standard forms (invoices, sales slips, purchase orders), and you'll save time and money using them for now.

WHAT'S WHAT IN BUSINESS

CATEGORIES	ADVANTAGES	DISADVANTAGES	COMMENTS
SOLE PROPRIETOR-SHIP	This is the simplest, least expensive way to form a business. It puts control, responsibility, and profits in the hands of a single person. Little or no governmental approval is required, and you can make decisions quickly, without consulting others.	You are personally liable for business debts. If sued, you could lose your personal assets as well as those of your business. Raising substantial investment capital is difficult. Your sickness, disability, or death will end the business.	Many people start out with this form of business, and take a partner or incorporate if expansion becomes desirable.
PARTNERSHIP	A co-owner, presumably someone you trust and respect, shares the work of running the business and offers ideas and counsel. With a partner, you have access to more capital; if you lose money, the loss is shared.	Profits must be shared with your partner. You and your partner are still personally liable for business debts; you also are liable for the business debts of your partner. Disagreements may be hard to resolve, slowing key decisions. Death or disablement of one partner will dissolve the partnership.	Not all partnerships follow the 50/50 model. Profits and work loads may be split in any percentage, but there should be a written agreement to that effect. A good lawyer is a must to help you draw up a written agreement.
CORPORATION	Your liability is limited, usually to the amount of your investment in company stock. This protects your personal assets. Investment capital is usually easier for a corporation to secure than for an individual.	This is the most costly and complicated form of business to start. It's closely regulated by the government, making careful record keeping and reporting a must. In some cases, corporate income is doubly taxed (as earnings by the corporation and as dividend income to shareholders).	In some states, professionals such as physicians, lawyers, dentists, and engineers may form Professional Corporations (sometimes called Professional Associations). They're essentially like regular corporations, but do not limit personal liability to the same extent.
S CORPORATION (formerly Subchapter S Corporation)	When you incorporate your small business under this type of arrangement, you make it possible to treat business earnings as personal income, and eliminate the "double-taxation" bind of regular corporations.	To use this form of incorporation, your business must meet certain strict qualifications—among them that there are no more than 35 shareholders (you and your spouse count as one) and one class of stock, and only a limited amount of income from "passive" investments. Ask your lawyer for details.	This is an option worth exploring, because it may provide tax relief.

MONEY MATTERS

You may have ideas in your head, a business plan in your briefcase, and reasonable expectations that clients will soon be on your doorstep. But if you don't have financing, you aren't ready to do business. Those who expect to be taken seriously in a home business must manage their money with care and skill. So read on to learn about loans, brush up on the basics of borrowing, and find out how financial statements can provide you with a quick fix on your financial status. You can't afford to ignore money matters. They are, quite literally, the bottom line of any business.

Money—borrowing it, collecting it, and managing it—is instrumental to any business's success. Planning and familiarity with basic financial principles make all three steps easier. When you formulate your business plan, carefully detail all anticipated expenses for starting up your operation.

Be sure to include the initial cost of licenses and permits, office furniture and equipment, and decorating and remodeling your work area, as well as fees for professional consultations. Then, figure out what it will cost to do business on a monthly basis, including fixed expenses such as utilities, insurance, and taxes, and variable expenses such as supplies, repairs and maintenance, and advertising. Remember, you'll have to carry these costs during that early period when your business is not yet profitable.

As a rule of thumb, experts suggest having enough capital in reserve to cover your start-up costs, plus your basic cost of business operations for

three to six months. Remember that you must allow for personal living expenses, too. If you don't have that much on hand, you'll need to borrow. Most financial institutions will expect you to supply as much as 50 percent or more of the total needed to launch your business.

Borrowing basics

Before financial institutions will lend you money, they look for indications that you are a good credit risk. They review your credit history, analyze your current assets, check current conditions and the general outlook for your industry, and determine whether you have any collateral, or security, to back up your ability to repay the loan. They also compare your net worth with the projected debt, and look at your projected cash flows and profit-and-loss projections to see whether

you'll be able to meet the repayment schedule. Other evaluations are more subjective. Does the loan officer think your business plan reflects both creativity and hard-nosed business sense? Do you convey a professional attitude? Do you seem capable and trustworthy? The answers to these questions can make a difference, so it pays to rehearse your presentation carefully.

It also pays to come prepared. Bring your neatly typed plan, plus a personal résumé, financial statements (see page 101), and profit forecasts. Having your loan application forms filled out in advance is also smart.

Commercial banks are a good source of capital, but

don't overlook other sources. You might also check into loans from credit unions, friends, or relatives, and, in the form of home mortgages, loans from savings and loan institutions. Perhaps you can borrow against your life insurance policy.

If you've been turned down by two commercial credit sources, you are eligible to apply for an SBA loan. SBA lending criteria may be more favorable for a start-up business than other sources are. Most SBA loans—about 90 percent of them—are in the form of guarantees on loans made by a lender such as a bank, although under certain conditions the SBA does make direct loans. Many different types of SBA programs exist, so check with your local SBA office to see what's available.

Collecting funds

Once your business is launched, your attention shifts from getting loans to getting paid. The battle here is proving to customers and clients that your home-based venture is indeed a business, not the dabblings of a half-baked hobbyist. Demonstrate this fact by acting like a professional; keep regular hours, have a separate business phone, provide written estimates for jobs, and draw up contracts that outline prices and conditions. Send out invoices promptly, and specify when payment is due. Follow up with a second invoice noting a past-due balance if you do not receive payment on schedule. Make it clear that like any serious businessperson, you expect to be paid on time.

Financial statements

Every business needs statements to indicate its current financial status. To help you analyze your business's finances, you should organize data into two generally accepted forms.

• *Balance sheet.* This tells you how much you own (assets) and how much you owe (liabilities). It reflects this information as of a given date, so many call it a "point in time" statement.

• *Income statement.* Also called a "P & L"—profit and loss—statement, this form tells you how much money you've brought in (income) and how much you've paid out (expenses) over a given period of time. You should generate financial statements regularly: for beginners, monthly is best. If you don't keep careful and frequent track of income and expenses, you may find yourself over your head financially before you even realize your business is in trouble. Your accountant can help you get the hang of putting together a periodic financial statement.

LEGAL MATTERS

"Don't you know it's the law?" This question can strike terror in the hearts of new home business owners. Having decided that legal issues are the province of experts, they may have failed to fully explore their responsibilities in the areas of zoning, licensing, insurance, and taxes. If you are in business for yourself, it's your job to make sure you're operating in accordance with local, state, and federal laws. A lawyer can advise you, but the ultimate duty for compliance rests with you. Another reason to know the law: When you're familiar with its workings, you can take advantage of the protections it offers small business owners.

When you choose to work out of your home, you need to consider how the community, state, and federal government will view that choice. They may require you to register your business, operate it only in a specific location, adhere to certain codes, obtain licenses or permits, and pay appropriate taxes. Failure to abide by any of these regulations can jeopardize your business.

About zoning
Your community can control where certain types of businesses are located. This power is reflected in zoning ordinances or laws, and may be backed by the government's ability to grant or withhold licenses or permits. Local government also sets building codes, which specify the physical structure of the place of business. If you're remodeling your home to accommodate your business, the changes must be in accordance with the local code. You'll probably have to undergo an inspection to show authorities that provisions of the code have been met.

In some areas, zoning is strictly enforced and home occupations are closely monitored. In other locales, little attention is paid to home-based workers, especially if they operate quietly and without noticeable effect on the surrounding neighborhood. But as more and more people make their homes their workplaces, communities are expected to regulate home businesses more stringently.

Before setting up your business, check with your local planning commission, building department, or board of supervisors to see if there are any restrictions you should know about. Many communities prohibit signs, and others stipulate that anyone who visits your home for business purposes must have an off-street parking space. In some areas, only members of the immediate family are allowed to serve as employees.

The community may ban outright business activities that generate noise (such as a recording studio), traffic (retail sale of crafts), or excessive sewage (dog grooming business). More often, however, there's room for a certain amount of interpretation in such regulations.

Licensing and permits
Do you need a license or permit to operate legally out of your home? It depends on the kind of business you're in. Some professionals, such as cosmetologists, contractors, and insurance adjusters, must be licensed in all states. They are usually tested to prove their competency as a condition of licensing. Other types of businesses require licenses or permits in certain communities, but not in others.

Much depends on local, county, and state ordinances. Some places require a "doing business at home" (DBA) license, for which you must register your business's name. If you're unsure about licensing requirements in your area, check with your lawyer, town administrator, or other home-based business people.

Idea protection
Some of the most valuable assets of your home business are your good ideas. The law makes it possible for you to "insure" your rights to their use through trademarks, copyrights, and patents.

• *Trademarks.* If you come up with a word, phrase, name, or symbol that signifies your business or product in a distinctive way, you can apply to have it registered with the Patent and Trademark Office of the Department of Commerce. First, have your lawyer ascertain that no one else is currently using the mark. Then, be sure you use it often and correctly in written documents; never use it as a verb.

• *Copyrights.* If you create an original artistic work (including a novel, play, painting, sculpture, or musical piece), you can protect its use and distribution with a copyright. Submit the finished work to the Register of Copyrights at the Library of Congress for registration. Or, if you publish a written work, include the © copyright notice, date of publication, and your name on the title page. For more information, contact the Register of Copyrights.

• *Patents.* These are the government's mechanism for protecting an individual's technical discovery. They guarantee inventors exclusive use of their invention—which may be either a product or a process—for 17 years. If you're working to develop an invention, keep detailed, dated notes on your experiment, signed and witnessed by a friend. Consult a patent attorney when you're ready to patent your design, because the process itself is involved. (Note: It's also expensive.)

Paying taxes
Your tax obligations as a home-based or self-employed businessperson are probably more complex than your

obligations would be if you were in a standard workplace and work situation. Work with an accountant at first to make sure you're paying the right kinds of taxes at the right time of year.

The taxes you owe depend upon your legal form of organization, the requirements of your state and local government, and the nature of your business. These are the main categories you need to consider.

• *Income tax.* This is tax paid to the federal, state, or local government on your business income. You must file a return annually. If your earnings exceed a set amount, you must pay estimated tax "as you go," usually quarterly.

• *Self-employment tax.* This is the social security tax for people who work for themselves: sole proprietors, farmers, or partners. It is also a pay-as-you-go tax.

• *Employment taxes.* If you employ others in your business, you must pay certain employment taxes. These include federal withholding taxes, social security (FICA) tax, and federal unemployment (FUTA) tax.

• *Excise taxes.* Those involved in certain occupations (manufacturing firearms, tires, and lubricating oil, for example) must pay federal excise tax. Ask your accountant if you are liable for these taxes.

• *Sales taxes.* Sales taxes are levied by most states. If you sell items in your business, you need to register that fact with the state. You then act as their agent, collecting taxes and passing them on.

EVALUATING INSURANCE

Every business enterprise involves risks. Having the right kinds of insurance won't eliminate those risks, but it will help protect you when conditions outside your control threaten your business's stability. A reputable insurance agent, broker, or consultant can advise you about the amount and type of coverage you need; first, however, you should take a good look at your business situation, deciding which perils to insure against and how much loss you might suffer from each. Experts say you should cover your largest loss exposure first, and take as high a deductible as you can afford. Another hint: Try to get all your insurance from a single agent, and be candid with that person about your business and its potential risks.

Here are some categories of insurance to consider.

• *Fire insurance.* Because a standard fire policy pays you only for losses directly caused by fire, you may want to add a "consequential loss" clause that covers some related losses (the added expense of moving to temporary quarters, for instance). You also can add protection from other perils to your policy: lightning, windstorm, hail, explosions, and vandalism.

• *Liability insurance.* Your homeowner's policy probably has a personal liability clause, but as a business owner, you may need a commercial liability policy. This will protect you and your company against most claims filed by employees or customers who consider you liable for their bodily injuries. You also can get specific coverage for personal injury (libel or slander, for instance), and product liability.

• *Auto insurance.* Business cars or trucks should be insured for collision, as well as liability. Experts suggest that you buy your automobile policies from the same company that insures your overall liability. If you have employees who drive their own cars on business, you may need "nonowned" auto liability coverage.

• *Crime insurance.* Comprehensive crime policies cover burglary, robbery, and other losses, including employee theft. If you have an alarm system, premiums will be lower.

• *Workers' compensation.* Most states require that you cover your employees under this program, which protects workers who are injured on the job. Rates for this insurance vary, depending on whether the job your employees do is considered hazardous or safe. (Coverage that pays when someone suffers disability unrelated to work is called disability insurance.)

• *Business interruption insurance.* When a fire or other calamity closes your business, you still have expenses (utilities, taxes, and interest, for example) to pay. This policy covers them for a specified time.

• *Extra expenses insurance.* If your customers depend on you for uninterrupted service (perhaps you publish a weekly newsletter, for instance), you may need this coverage. It makes sure you have money to continue your business after a disaster such as a fire.

• *Key-employee insurance.* The success of a small business can be extremely dependent on a particular employee. If so, it may make sense for the business to insure that employee's life and continued health.

• *Retirement.* You can get tax deductions for purchasing annuity or insurance contracts approved for use under the Employees Retirement Income Security Act of 1974 (ERISA). Ask your insurance agent for details.

One final note: Even if you think your homeowner's insurance is adequate for your business needs, check with your agent. In some cases, you void your homeowner's policy by working in your home.

KEEPING BOOKS

Granted, you must keep accurate records if you expect to identify and meet your tax obligations. But well-kept books also can help you make better business decisions. When you know what you've spent and what is due you, it is easier to gauge your present financial situation and plan logically for the future.

The most common system for keeping the books of a small business is "double-entry" bookkeeping, so called because it requires you to register every business transaction twice. Unlike its single-entry counterpart, this form of bookkeeping is self-balancing.

For every transaction, a dated entry reflecting both the debit (value received) and credit (value parted with) aspect should be entered in your journal. The debit column and the credit column must balance for each entry.

On a regular basis (monthly, for most people), summary totals of the journal entries are transferred onto *ledger accounts* in a process called *posting*. During posting, you are consolidating daily transactions under logical headings, but you still maintain the balance of debits and credits established in your journal. To provide a good overview, ledger accounts are generally divided into categories, usually one each for income, expenses, cost of sales, assets, liabilities, and net worth. Ledger accounts can eventually be used to generate financial statements (see pages 100 and 101).

Identifying deductions

Your tax liabilities as a home-based worker can be lightened if you take advantage of legitimate deductions. Don't think of this as a questionable practice. Any IRS official will tell you the government considers it your right to use all possible saving measures, as long as you are accurate in your reporting and interpretation.

Be sure to explore the possibility of "writing off" certain expenses associated with using your home as your place of business. Before you are considered eligible for these deductions, you must meet certain stringent requirements. The most basic ones involve exclusive and regular use of your home. Tax laws and regulations tend to change often, so be sure to check the present rules.

• *Exclusive use.* Taxpayers must use a designated room or area in their home solely for business purposes. You cannot, for instance, use a corner of your bedroom as your design studio and write off the entire room; you may only write off the percentage of it (in square feet) used exclusively for business. The only exceptions to this rule involve storage of inventory and use of your home as a day-care facility.

• *Regular use.* You must use your home as a place of business on a continuing basis, not occasionally or incidentally.

In a related area, the IRS also insists that your home be your principal place of business if you are to qualify for

deductions. You can, however, have more than one principal place of business if you have more than one job or business. That means full-time employees can still qualify for deductions if they run a part-time business not connected with their other job from their home.

Other factors that affect how the IRS views your home-based business activities include whether you need your home as a place to meet patients, clients, or customers; whether you maintain a free-standing structure (studio, garage, or barn) exclusively for business; whether you are engaged in a trade or business (rather than a profit-seeking activity, such as personal research to help your stock trading activities); and, if you are an employee, whether you maintain a home office for the convenience of your employer.

If you meet the regular and exclusive use tests and any of the conditions noted above, you're most likely eligible for certain deductions.

It is possible to deduct both *direct expenses* (the cost of painting your office, for instance) and parts of some *indirect expenses*. In any case, your deductions for use of

your home as your office cannot exceed the gross income from the business use of your home. A good accountant can help you get the maximum tax relief you're due.

Finally, a reminder that there is a valuable tax credit that home-based workers may inadvertently overlook: the child-care credit. This applies to expenses incurred in caring for your child, a disabled dependent, or a disabled spouse, and is available to you no matter where you work.

Any company name and address used in this section are purely fictitious. Any similarity to an actual business concern is strictly coincidental.

PERSONNEL AND EQUIPMENT

Today, home-based workers seldom fit the image of the proverbial solitary struggler or lonely, starving artist. Instead, they've discovered the value of help, be it in the form of people or equipment. Many contract with or employ others on a part-time, full-time, or as-needed basis. Others may be part of a larger industry, and simply choose to perform their share of the work at home. To lighten their load of routine tasks, many individuals are investing in computers, smart typewriters, and photocopying machines. The result of all these changes? Increased productivity, greater job satisfaction, and a more professional image for home business owners.

More and more people who work at home are discarding the notion that they must do everything themselves. As their businesses grow, they may find it feasible (and economically favorable) to hire outside help. Depending on space availability and zoning requirements, they may choose to bring others into their homes to perform the needed tasks, or arrange to have the work done elsewhere. In any case, they take on a new set of responsibilities when they become employers.

Help wanted
At some point, you may feel that you can no longer run your home business by yourself. Perhaps you find yourself falling behind, working too many nights and weekends, or having to turn away clients because there's no time to service them. Additional help might prove valuable. It may take several forms.

First, take a look at the kinds of tasks you perform daily, and analyze what you can readily delegate to others. If you're spending lots of time typing or answering routine phone calls, a secretarial or answering service might be the solution. If running errands is taking you away from more important tasks, a messenger service might provide welcome relief. Maybe you spend too much time cleaning your work area, when a cleaning service could be doing the job more effectively. If you hire services for such tasks, you simply pay to have certain jobs performed and don't have to worry about employee benefits.

In other cases, you'll decide that you need another employee. This is a major step away from being an independent, home-based businessperson—you are becoming an employer, with all the responsibility that entails. Before you search for an appropriate person, write a job description for the position you plan to fill. Outline activities the new employee will be expected to perform, and list skills the person should have. Hiring then becomes a process of matching what the candidate has to offer with your specific needs.

You can find potential employees in a number of ways. Check with nearby high schools or community colleges for students interested in part-time or summer work. Register the job with a government or private employment agency. Place classified ads in your local paper, or post a notice on bulletin boards at churches, shopping centers, or community houses. If you need workers with a specific skill, you might contact trade and professional associations for leads. Word of mouth is another possibility.

All job applicants should fill out an application (forms are available at most stationery stores), listing their education, work history, and pertinent personal data. When you interview an applicant, use the form as a jumping-off point for questions. But remember: You cannot discriminate against a potential employee on the basis of race, sex, religion, color, or national origin. That means your questions should revolve around the applicant's ability to do the job, and not focus on these other issues. During the interview, take time to review the job description, the hours, and the pay scale. Ask for several references, and be sure to check them.

Once you've settled on the person you want to hire, you take on several new obligations in your role as employer. Some are simply common sense: your implied obligation to orient and train the new employee, for instance. Others are more complex, and are enforced by law.

Employment taxes
You may need some help in understanding your legal duties as an employer—specifically, your tax obligations. An accountant or lawyer should be consulted to ensure proper compliance, but here are the basics.

• *Income tax withholding.* Most business owners with at least one employee are required to withhold federal income tax from the employee's wages. You'll need an employer identification number (get an application from the IRS or the Social Security Administration), and your employee will have to fill out a Form W-4, noting the exemptions he or she claims. The form also gives you the right to withhold the proper taxes, and pay them to the government on your employee's behalf. (Note: You'll probably have to withhold state and local taxes as well. Check to be sure.)

• *Social security taxes.* With these taxes (also called FICA taxes, for Federal Insurance Contributions Act), you both deduct money on your employee's behalf and add a matching sum because you are the employer. You must deposit the total sum for a set period in a Federal Reserve bank or other authorized institution. You must have your employee's social security number to make these deposits.

• *Federal unemployment tax (FUTA).* This is money earmarked for the protection of workers against complete loss of income when work is not available. If you pay your employees more than a set amount, you must pay this tax (perhaps at the state level as well) on their wages; employees do not contribute themselves. Make deposits at a Federal Reserve bank or other authorized institution.

Safe conditions
Ensuring your employees' safety also ensures your own; there are legal as well as ethical and practical requirements to consider.
• *General safety measures.* By law, you must supply your employees with a safe workplace. This includes providing safe tools, hiring competent fellow employees, and warning employees of any existing dangers.
• *Workers' compensation insurance.* State laws almost always require that you provide this insurance for your employees, protecting them in the case of disabilities incurred on the job. Premiums are paid to an authorized insurance agency, based on the risk assigned to your employee's job.

Other working arrangements
Sometimes, you will pay individuals for their work, but the government will not technically consider you their employer. Your legal obligations may be different in these cases. You may, for instance, pay a royalty for their creative work. If the payment exceeds a set amount, you would be required to file Form 1099-MISC, the Statement for Recipients of Miscellaneous Income, with the IRS. You also would have to

file this form if you paid someone certain fees or commissions. Check with your accountant for details.

Another possibility in some businesses is for the owner to contract with other individuals to complete certain tasks (writing a brochure, or designing a logo, for instance) for a set fee. If the task involves the creation of a work, the one commissioning it may want to draw up a "work-for-hire" agreement, which both parties should agree to and sign. Essentially, this agreement states that the one who commissions and pays for a work is considered the initial copyright owner. (In standard employee-employer situations, works prepared by employees in the course of their jobs are considered works for hire automatically.)

One fast-growing trend in the work-at-home phenomenon is known as the cottage industry, a system in which several individuals produce items in their homes, supplying them to a central distributor for final marketing. The practice is highly controversial, fostering much disagreement about the central distributor's obligations to those who produce the items, issues of minimum wage and child labor, and, in some areas, the legality of the worker being engaged in crafts-making for someone else's profit at home.

If you are interested in doing this type work where you live, experts suggest you first discuss the arrrangements with the Labor Department's Wage and Hour Division in your area. The representative should be able to tell you how a cottage industry is viewed by your community in terms of zoning, licensing, and labor laws.

EQUIPMENT

You're starting your own business, and decide you need a car, a computer, a typewriter, or a photocopying machine to enable you to perform in the most efficient manner. After settling on the model you want, you're faced with the question: Should you lease or purchase it?

As with many tough business questions, there are no easy answers. The answer that's right for you depends on a number of factors, including your cash flow, your need for predictability, whether you're considered a good enough credit prospect to qualify for a lease, and your willingness to live with risk.

Leasing involves paying a fixed fee on a monthly or annual basis for the use of an item for a set period. You may be required to pay an additional fee upon the inauguration of the leasing agreement as security.

When your lease is up, you do not own the item; it remains the property of the lessor. If your agreement calls for a lease with an option to buy, however, you may be able to purchase the item when your lease is up.

Leasing fees are considered expenses, and, as such, they are easily deductible if they relate to your business. The government allows you to write off the cost of the lease as an

annual expense, making the bookkeeping aspects of leasing rather simple.

Some leases provide for maintenance of the item. In this instance, the lessor will either repair the equipment or replace it with another machine. Many people like this kind of freedom from responsibility, but keep in mind that a maintenance contract is only as good as the service department that's providing the maintenance. Know the reputation of your lessor or agent.

Purchasing is just what you'd expect: buying an item outright. When you purchase an item that is business related, it becomes one of your business assets. Of course, it ties up some of your capital, too.

The government allows you to depreciate a certain percentage of some large business purchases on a schedule, based on the perceived decline in their value over a period of years. This involves some extensive computations, and some people prefer the relative ease of leasing deductions. Maintenance is another issue to consider. If you buy an item, maintaining it is up to you. You can purchase service contracts for an additional sum, however, and warranties may cover you for a time. Be sure to weigh such pros and cons for every purchase or lease arrangement you evaluate.

MARKETING YOUR BUSINESS

In today's competitive world, it takes proper marketing to create the excitement that creates sales. If you're tempted to gloss over this phase because you're home based, think again. You of all people need the professional polish to dispel any lingering doubts about your work. From presentation and pricing to advertising and promoting, good marketing shows the world you're a pro who deserves a pay scale to match.

Creating what experts sometimes call "the marketing mix"—just the right combination of pricing, product, and promotion— is one of the keys to running a profitable home business. A common mistake for new business owners is to devote all their energies to developing a salable product or service, and leave pricing and promotion to chance. Don't fall into that trap.

Pricing decisions

Setting a good price is almost an art form. You must take many factors into consideration, including what your competition charges, how your target customers react to pricing, the current state of the economy, and how much it costs you to produce your product or deliver your service.

You must then strike that precarious balance between overpricing and underpricing. Especially during the important start-up phase, too high a price can make people dismiss you out of hand. If your price is too low, however, you tend to devalue what you have to offer.

The goal of good pricing should be to help your business become or stay profit-

able. To that end, you should keep detailed records of your costs, because all expenses must be figured in to the final price of your product. Remember to include what you spend on materials, as well as a percentage of your overhead (utilities and supplies, for example). Be sure to charge for the cost of your own labor, at no less than the minimum wage. And don't forget to add on extra to guarantee you'll make a profit. There's no point being in business if you lose sight of this motive.

Promotion pays off

Promotion is another key marketing tool. Think of it as a way to communicate ideas and images that can build the image of your product or company in

the eyes of potential customers. It can take several forms—advertising, publicity (or public relations), sales promotion, or a combination of these.

• *Advertising.* Chances are good you're already familiar with the goal of advertising: to promote your business through paid messages directed at your target customers. But perhaps you've decided your initial budget is too low to allow you to advertise. True, some of the media favored by large companies are probably out of reach. Still, your target customers may be reachable by other means.

Consider small ads in your local newspaper, Yellow Pages display ads, or flyers distributed in your area. Can you afford a small radio spot or an ad in a specialty magazine? Does your business lend itself to promotion via direct mail? All of these are possibilities to explore.

Sometimes, ads also carry a certain public relations value. Such is the case with good will messages you can run in high school yearbooks, church bulletins, or community celebration publications. These ads are generally inexpensive, and worth considering.

• *Publicity.* This is an area of marketing that's often misunderstood. You'll sometimes hear it called "free advertising," but that label is slightly inaccurate. When you run an ad, you control its contents totally, ensuring the message will be favorable to you. You have no real control over publicity; the media print or broadcast whatever they choose. Your influence stops short of control.

The most basic way to get publicity is to keep in touch with your local media. Newspaper reporters and broadcast journalists are constantly searching for a good story. If your business is the first of its type in your area, or you're planning a special demonstration or celebration, the media may be interested. A short press release should be sent to alert them to such opportunities.

• *Sales promotion.* The term "sales promotion" covers a wide range of activities, from discounts and special displays to contests and giveaways (T-shirts, pencils, memo pads) that carry your business's name. One easy-to-implement form of sales promotion for business owners getting their companies off the ground is sampling potential customers.

Making a statement
Obviously, you make a statement with your ads, press releases, or promotional materials. Don't forget that you also create an image with your stationery and business cards. Most printers offer a good choice of standard letterheads, in enough type styles and colors to appeal to a number of tastes. When you have the proper supplies, you signal to customers that you are serious about your pursuit. And that's precisely the image that those who work at home must strive to convey.

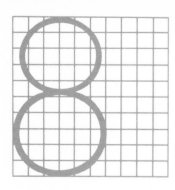

AT-HOME OFFICES

For many people, an at-home office is everything an office anywhere else would be—a full-fledged, full-time workplace. For others, it's a retreat for doing highly concentrated work free of main-office distractions and bustle. And for still others, a home office offers a way to remain professionally active, yet be in close touch with children and household routines. For all of the individuals in this chapter, an at-home office means business; each provides an opportunity for combining professional-quality work with the convenience and flexibility of being at home on the job.

THE INTERIOR DESIGNER

For an interior designer who helps other people decorate their homes, what could be more sensible than working out of an office in her own home? Aside from the usual working-at-home advantages, such as saved commuting time and flexible workdays, the home office shown here creates an informal yet thoroughly businesslike atmosphere in which to exchange ideas and make plans.

Because interior design is not a high-traffic business and requires small-scale—though numerous—materials, such as swatches and sample books, setting up an office on the main floor of the designer's home presented no difficulties and violated no zoning regulations. The designer simply took over space in what was once the family room.

The parsons table, with its clean, uncluttered lines, provides abundant work space. Because the table has no self-enclosed storage, the wall behind it is equipped as a storage unit and secondary work surface. When meeting with clients, the designer sits at the table, facing them in the standard office host/visitor arrangement. When working alone, however, she often uses the built-in wall desk, which offers ready access to shelves, drawers, and closets.

Lightweight wicker chairs combine front-porch charm with easy mobility. The one near the tree can be shifted to face the parsons table during conferences; the one behind the table works equally well at the other desk. These chairs, along with the ceiling beams and deep-tone wood floor, also add warmth and texture to an otherwise monochromatic, smooth-surface setting.

AT-HOME OFFICES

THE ARCHITECT

Wherever they work, architects are likely to have a strong sense of place; it's their job, after all, to consider buildings from aesthetic, practical, and engineering perspectives. It's not always possible for architects to practice exclusively at home. Much of their work involves visits to planned building sites, for example. But for other parts of the job, a home office is ideal because it can provide flexible office hours, solitude when necessary, and the personalized surroundings conducive to creative effort.

The architect's aerie pictured *at right* is an office away from the office. Well-planned and heavily used, this work area, which the architect shares with his sewing-hobbyist wife, was originally an unfinished attic. The owner remodeled it to provide home work space when he felt the pressures of long hours at his main office were excessive.

To bring light and passive solar gain to the area, the architect added a 2-foot-deep bump-out greenhouse window. A circular window, not shown, was placed at the peak of the roof; besides bringing in extra light, it serves as an intriguing architectural accent for the area.

The work surface, which is 12 feet long, is attached to the knee wall, occupying space that might otherwise be wasted because of its lack of headroom. Three file cabinets serve as both storage pieces and supports for the shared work surfaces. One of the cabinets is a standard metal model; the other two are wooden file-and-drawer combinations from an unpainted furniture store.

Although certain features of the work space, such as the tilt-top drafting table, are specifically geared for design work, many other elements of this attic office are more general in purpose. An articulated clamp-on lamp provides efficient task lighting; low-pile carpet softens sounds and goes well with the dark-brown ceiling trim and natural wood strip ceiling. Lightweight metal desk chairs are comfortable and easy to move; their bright blue cushions provide cheerful color accents and pick up the classic shade of architects' blueprints.

THE GRAPHIC DESIGNER

Graphic designers determine what printed products look like; they select type, layouts, and artwork. The design process itself may be solitary, but it's important to discuss goals with clients first. For this reason, a designer either spends some time in other people's offices or sets aside an area for conferences at home.

The well-equipped basement design studio pictured *below* and the comfortable viewing room shown *at left* enable a full-time working mother to maintain professional credibility while remaining within reach of her two young children. The owner of this studio found it took some extra initial effort to convince clients that her business was a serious one, despite its home address. She believes, however, that home offices are ideal for anyone who can work in one place and have the results shown in another, such as a gallery, publication, or client's headquarters.

Because the graphic design business is considered what zoning boards often call a "gentleman's practice"—that is, no exterior sign, no big trucks, no neighborhood disruption—the homeowner did not have to seek a variance to establish her business.

Thanks to a sensible renovation, visitors can enter the office directly from the driveway, through an attractive new glass door. A separate telephone line helps keep home and work life from overlapping.

THE DENTIST

Because medical and dental offices typically generate considerable traffic, require extra parking spaces, and remain open for extended hours, they are usually subject to zoning regulations and may be relegated to main arteries in suburban areas. What's more, patients have an easier time finding a main-street office. The dentist's office featured here achieves an ideal balance between easy access and privacy.

For a dentist just starting out in practice, finding—and funding—both a home and an office can be difficult. The dentist whose at-home office is shown here solved the problem creatively by purchasing a two-story house on a busy street zoned for mixed residential and commercial use.

The lower level of the building, not visible from the street, is where the dentist lives; a separate entrance at the rear provides privacy. The structure's upper level was remodeled to serve as a full-service dental office. Except for a bay added to provide one more room in the professional quarters, the basic outline of the house remained the same, with the addition of some new exterior materials to help create a rustic, woodsy look.

As the photo *below* shows, the office's exterior presents a thoroughly professional face to the street, and the new redwood siding and cedar roof shingles add a pleasantly restful quality. To accommodate patients' cars, the dentist designed off-street parking for up to 10 vehicles. Well-planned low-maintenance landscaping—also his own creation—again achieves a balance between aesthetic appeal and professional efficiency.

Inside, the upstairs space shows more evidence of its new role. The original kitchen was converted into a dental lab, using existing plumbing and fixtures; the new downstairs home kitchen lines up directly below it, resulting in plumbing savings. The waiting room is the original living room, complete with fireplace.

The examining room pictured *opposite* occupies what was once bedroom space— two bedrooms, in fact. The wall between the two rooms was replaced by a storage divider, making supplies and equipment accessible to both the room shown here and the matching one on the other side of the divider. Sink and counter space are conveniently located along the inner wall in each examining room, so patients can face the windows and enjoy a relaxing view of wooded hills.

Here, all the necessary furnishings fit into a carefully conceived overall plan that combines up-to-the-minute dental apparatus with low-key decorative accents, such as the clerestory stained-glass panels and old-style ceiling fan/light fixtures.

THE LAWYER

Law is anything but a monolithic profession. Lawyers can be found in giant corporations, government agencies, small partnerships, and solo practices, among other settings. The practice of law doesn't always lend itself to working at home, the popular image of the small-town lawyer's office on a tree-lined street notwithstanding. That doesn't mean it can't be done, though, and with the help of computer networks, shifts in population, and determination, a lawyer can still hang out his or her shingle at home.

At first glance, there's nothing to indicate that the thoroughly professional-looking law office pictured *at right* is in a home. It has the office furnishings, wood paneling, and vertical blinds you'd associate with a standard corporate work space. But that careful attention to efficient detail and atmosphere is all part of a conscientious effort to keep a home law office well within the realm of professionalism.

Any law office has certain basic needs. These include a generously dimensioned desk for the lawyer to work at, a waiting area for clients, a conference table with comfortable seating, a work station for a secretary, and the physical bases for confidentiality and security—fireproof files and a safe. A separate entrance lets clients come and go without disrupting family activities.

Computers have come to law offices, too. Computer networks put information about countless cases literally at the fingertips of lawyers throughout the country. Though the cost of subscribing to these services may be beyond the reach of small firms and solo practitioners, these research networks are compatible with the word processors used to type briefs and other day-to-day materials, so there's always the potential of hooking in later.

Because they generate traffic in greater volume than would normally occur in a residential area, law offices usually come under the same zoning regulations as other professional offices. In rural areas, there may be no zoning; in suburbs and small towns, law offices may be limited to homes on major arteries. For more about zoning, see page 102.

THE VIDEO SPECIALIST

Working as a video specialist isn't all games, though it's often fun. Whether the video material in question is a 60-second commercial, a syndicated television program, or a series of documentaries designed for classroom use, there's more than glamour involved in their production. The work lends itself to independence, and to using home as a base, because creative "quiet" time and preliminary research are often needed to prepare the video package. To succeed in this high-gloss, high-tech field, you have to be familiar with electronic media equipment, marketing strategies, audience needs, and more. A well-set-up office, whether at home or elsewhere, is a good place to start.

The media room pictured *at right* belongs to a self-employed video specialist who prepares television commercials, hosts a local television program, and serves as a consultant for producers of video materials. A good part of his work is done in a television studio or at clients' offices. He also spends a good amount of time in his home office, planning, writing, and researching, using his own library as a resource center.

Because the office is used for meetings as well as individual work sessions, size and appearance are important. This 12x18-foot space was once a ground-floor bedroom; thanks to its furnishings and skillfully designed storage arrangements, it looks like the kind of well-windowed corner office most business people would like to have. The furniture is office furniture, pure and simple. A leather armchair facing the main work desk (matched by a love seat, not shown) lends a touch of luxury, but the overall effect is, as intended, thoroughly businesslike.

Lateral files extending from the doorway to the corner provide closed storage for tapes. They also serve as a level surface for the assorted sound and video equipment so important in this field. Another lateral file cabinet, behind the desk, is topped by well-filled bookshelves.

The desk is larger than most. Besides providing plenty of room for the telephone and typewriter, it offers ample work space and temporary storage for books or tapes that are needed for the day's work.

Restful, undistracting white walls and a rich brown carpet that muffles household sounds are carefully planned design features. An unadorned wall opposite the desk, not shown, is ideal for showing films and slides, and vertical blinds at the large window behind the desk can be closed to block out daylight during showings.

Setting up a media room

There's a wealth of electronic equipment to be found in a professional-level video center. The television set that might serve a recreational or background-sound purpose in other home offices is a necessary tool of the trade here. Other equipment and accessories include VCRs, audio tape decks, record players, and slide and movie projectors.

Clearly, electricity is a key concern, and well-planned outlets—lots of them and in the right places—are necessities. Wires stretching along the floor can be hazardous as well as unsightly.

In addition to the practical matter of finding room and connections for all of the necessary equipment, consider comfort, too. Make sure that seating is comfortable enough to sit in while watching screenings for long periods of time, and faces the right direction—or can be moved easily to face the right direction. Neck muscles suffer if the angle from chair to a monitor screen or screening wall is wrong.

Also plan storage carefully. The file system shown here works well, but many audio/video cabinets found in furniture stores would work equally well. These come in wood, metal, even glass or acrylic. In all cases, keep in mind that electronic equipment is sensitive to changes in temperature and humidity, so components should be stored away from heat and drafts and protected from excessive light.

A desk, a chair, and pen and paper may be all you *really* need to write even the Great American Novel, but for most writers, writing isn't just a spontaneous creative process. There's research to be done, assignments to be solicited, outlines to be made. Writers need storage for paper, shelves for books, counter space for typewriters or computers, and files—or computers—for record keeping. They need ways to communicate with the outside world, whether by telephone or computer, and a comfortable and presentable seating area for conferences, interviewing, or just relaxing between chapters, paragraphs, or, sometimes, sentences.

The writer's room shown on these two pages provides all the equipment and amenities a writer might want, and its own special charm as well. The solid oak rolltop desk, file cabinet, table, desk chair, and assorted side tables evoke the solid, steady mood of a turn-of-the-century law office. The desktop word processor, linked to the outside publishing world by the modem to its right, brings the writer right into the computer age.

Copy drafted at the rolltop desk and input on the computer can be transmitted hundreds of miles in seconds, and readied for typesetting in as much time as it once took just for a typed manuscript to arrive at its destination by mail.

Personalized but professional

This home office is somewhat unusual because of its location in a formerly industrial building that now houses residential lofts. (Other views of this loft are shown on pages 64 and 65.) High ceilings make it possible to use space vertically as well as horizontally—see the guest sleeping loft in the background of the photo *below.*

More important, and more generally applicable to any writer's home office, this room provides quiet, privacy, comfort, and plenty of room for resource materials. Track lights (not shown) provide general lighting; task lighting comes from an industrial-style dropped ceiling fixture and a period desk lamp. Sliding pocket doors can shut the office off from the main living area, but even with the doors closed, a transom above the doorway, visible in the photo *opposite,* provides a sense of openness that nicely balances the solid brick walls.

AT-HOME OFFICES

THE FIELD EDITOR

You may sometimes wonder how the varied and appealing homes pictured in decorating publications are discovered. It's true that sometimes a house is found by chance, just as a dazzling new movie star or model might be. But more often, finding material to photograph for a magazine or book is part of a time-consuming and ongoing process that involves not only the publication's in-house staff but a special group of people known as field editors. Their job is to keep track of building, remodeling, and decorating trends and actual projects in a given geographical area, considering almost every home or room they see as a possible candidate for photography.

The pleasant and compact office pictured *at left* belongs to a *Better Homes and Gardens*® field editor. Although hers is a specialized profession, her office would serve almost any home-based worker equally well. It also has several features that might appeal particularly to other people who both work at home and travel extensively, such as sales personnel.

After several years of using cramped basement quarters as her home office, this field editor decided to move upstairs and adapt the recently vacated bedroom of a college-age child to her own needs. She hoped to create an attractive, efficient, and unpretentious home office, without spending a lot of money.

Gray walls and white woodwork make economical use of the room's original decor. New overhead storage cabinets help turn the space into a "real" office and keep the desk area below free for work. Tucked between the main door and the closet door is a portable storage unit, with three drawers that swing out for access to office necessities such as paper clips and tape.

The computer is helpful in this office not just for word processing but also for keeping track of home visits, editors' requests, and more. The bookshelves house a library of decorating and building resources; the file cabinet and open drawer system in the closet (shown in the inset) contain slides, photographs, and magazine tear sheets. This careful organization makes it easy for the field editor to find background information right away if she wants to take reference materials along on a scouting or photographic expedition.

AT-HOME OFFICES

PLANNING AN AT-HOME OFFICE

If you're planning to establish a special-purpose professional facility such as a medical or dental office in your home, technical and legal considerations will determine much of what you do. At the other end of the at-home office spectrum are more solitary activities, such as writing or graphic design, where you have almost unlimited possibilities as long as you give yourself seating, desk room, and good lighting. Given the many variables, there are, nevertheless, a few basic considerations to keep in mind.

Traffic and noise
Whenever you are planning an office—and especially if you'll be having clients or colleagues in—be sure access to your office is set apart from access to your home's family zones.

Consider, too, investing in soundproofing. You probably don't want the laughter of children at play to interrupt a conference, and it's equally important that confidential business transactions not be overheard.

Organization
The drawing *at right* shows a complete all-purpose office suitable for anyone from a lawyer to an editor to a wardrobe consultant. It's in the specifics of furnishings and decor that the individual differences and needs of various home-based offices become apparent.

Some of the features suggested here may be more office than you need; others may be even more important to you than indicated in this illustration. For example, you might feel that you don't need the barrier of a locked door to separate your third-floor editorial office from the living areas of your home; on the

other hand, if there's an entrance to your office directly from outside, you might want a more substantial door and lock than the one pictured here.

Here are some additional pointers that apply to virtually any home office.

• Plan electrical outlets carefully to avoid spiderwebs of wires stretching from desk to outlet to table and back again. Also consider telephone and computer locations carefully, so that they're within reach of each other if necessary.

• Fluorescent lighting provides excellent illumination, but you may find the light unpleasant to work under or consider the look of most fluorescent fixtures too institutional. In place of the fluorescent fixture pictured here, you might choose incandescent ceiling fixtures supplemented by abundant task lighting.

• A rolling chair is best for sitting at a desk, but for conference seating, that degree of mobility isn't necessary—any fairly light-weight chair will do.

• The wooden floor suggested here is easy to keep clean under light to moderate use, and easy to roll a chair across. For a colorful accent, or in a space where flooring isn't wood, such as a garage, attic, or basement, you might want to consider carpeting. And for an office where spills and other damages are a possibility, durable resilient flooring or ceramic or quarry tile might be a better choice. Keep in mind, however, that hard-surface flooring can be noisy; again, you might want to add area rugs to serve as both decorative accents and sound softeners.

If you're planning to establish the kind of at-home business that involves clients, you'll want to take their comfort and convenience into account. Key considerations include direct access from the outside, a door lock to ensure privacy, a conference table for formal discussions, and casual seating for planning or get-acquainted sessions. Then add a few extras, if possible—a small refrigerator, a coffee pot, a toaster or microwave oven, and a water cooler, for example.

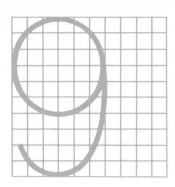

OTHER HOME-BASED BUSINESSES

An at-home workplace needn't be an office. In fact, a disinclination for desk work motivated many of the entrepreneurs profiled in this chapter to strike out on their own. From chefs to sheep ranchers and innkeepers, these home-based business people started out with something they enjoyed and parlayed their interests into profitable and personally satisfying ventures.

AN ANTIQUE BUSINESS

A longtime fondness for antique quilts and country furniture blossomed into a basement business for the owners of the antique shop pictured *below* and *opposite*. The partners, old friends who pooled their knowledge and energies, set up shop in a former playroom in one owner's home.

Because of the residential setting, they deal by appointment only, thus limiting customer traffic. No outside sign announces their business, but twice yearly they expand their clientele with public sales that last several days.

This arrangement also gives both women time to travel in search of merchandise. They attend auctions, house sales, and flea markets, and occasionally also visit other antique shops. One partner concentrates her efforts on the East Coast; the other scouts the Midwest. Their children, now grown and scattered around the country, also keep their eyes open for appealing additions to the inventory.

Although the partners had little previous business experience, they did have considerable expertise about antiques. Both had extensively furnished their own homes with vintage pieces and know an antique bargain when they see one. In addition, as avid quilters, they had learned about evaluating antique quilts and textiles.

Their shop deals strictly in country antiques, especially practical and affordable pine pieces, and one-of-a-kind quilts. Using a van and a station wagon, the women load the antiques themselves and carry them through an outside entrance to the basement showroom.

A STAINED-GLASS STUDIO

The owner of this studio and sales center gave up a nursing career when her interest in working with stained glass grew from a hobby into a profitable home business. She partitioned off two sections of her basement, one for working and the other for a showroom to sell finished pieces and hobby supplies. Zoning regulations in this semirural area prohibit excessive traffic and an untidy exterior, neither of which was a problem for this artisan.

For all their delicate beauty, the stained-glass windows pictured here are created in a decidedly utilitarian workshop. The main worktable, pictured *opposite,* is made of plain, unfinished plywood and can withstand the abuses of soldering guns and heating irons used to solder joints in the metal that secures the glass panels. In addition to the worktable, this artisan has a bench used only for grinding and polishing glass, and another workbench for making minor adjustments on wooden window frames. (She contracts out most of her framing work.)

Exposed fluorescent tubes provide plenty of light, and space between the ceiling joists houses rolls of lead came—the metal that holds together the panes in a stained-glass window—on dowels inserted in predrilled holes in the joists. Large glass-cutting tools such as triangles and straightedges also hang out of the way, suspended from the joists.

Lying flat on the worktable are sections of a 100-year-old church window, one of a series that the church has commissioned her to reshape to fit newly designed openings. The job entails unobtrusively blending old and new sections, matching colors, and reshaping pieces.

This artisan travels frequently throughout the Midwest to select individual pieces of glass, which she transports home in a van. Glass must be stored vertically; its own weight can break it in a horizontal position. One wall of the basement, along with space under the large worktable, is outfitted with upright bins for safe glass storage.

Turning glass into cash

Behind the worktable is a sales center, shown *above*. Here the stained-glass maker markets hobbyist supplies—pattern books, caming, glass, and tools—along with finished pieces. She also sells finished pieces at crafts fairs and by special request.

On the business side, the artisan says she floundered for a while trying to understand the mysteries of book and record keeping, then sought advice from the U.S. Small Business Administration (SBA). Through the SBA, she met with a representative of SCORE (the Service Corps of Retired Executives). He explained many of the basics presented in Chapter 7, and also guided her to an accountant who understands small businesses.

A COOKING SCHOOL

This kitchen is the heart of both family life and career for a cooking instructor who designed it to function smoothly in its dual role. Divided into three free-flowing sections, the 1,000-square-foot space accommodates an eating area, a seating area with fireplace, and a spacious cooking/teaching area. More than half a dozen students or dinner guests can comfortably gather around the center island for an unobstructed view of culinary demonstrations.

A teaching kitchen is more than just a home kitchen on a grand scale. The design of a home kitchen should maximize the comfort and efficiency of one or two cooks; the layout of a teaching kitchen must accommodate students, as well.

In the kitchen pictured *at right,* the teacher works on the right side of the island, with her work triangle of refrigerator, range, and sink arranged beside her, and seated students facing her. Their stools back up to a room-length counter (not shown) that mirrors the one under the windows but is 3 feet deep. The extra depth provides room for a variety of small appliances, such as a mixer, food processor, and grinder, frequently used for classes and home cooking.

Large aisles around the island leave ample room for students to work alongside the teacher or move in close to observe procedures. Sinks at each end of the room enable students to work separately, without crossing paths.

The kitchen has been outfitted with a combination of restaurant and household appliances. Installed in the center island, a restaurant range top features six burners and a 24-inch griddle. The hood was mounted high overhead to avoid blocking the students' views of demonstrations. (A pair of professional 36-inch ovens are just out of camera range at right.) An extra-large refrigerator fits flush with cabinetry; its wide, shallow design makes it easy to keep track of supplies.

In the seating area, a cozy fireplace also plays a utilitarian role. Designed for cooking, it features built-in irons and winches to support open-hearth cookware.

A CATERER'S KITCHEN

Do your chocolate chip cookies disappear as fast as you make them? Do guests give your dinner parties four-star reviews? If so, you may have wondered whether a wider public also would appreciate your efforts. Family recipes may require only a few changes, but turning your home kitchen into a professional catering operation means meeting restaurant health standards. Here, we present a home-caterer who scores high marks with both clients and health inspectors.

Passengers on the corporate jets serviced by this caterer never complain about having to eat airline food. Still-warm breakfast rolls greet early fliers, and later travelers choose from a tempting cold buffet.

Her kitchen, pictured *opposite,* doesn't look commercial, but it's been planned with businesslike efficiency. Ample counter space holds a variety of cooking utensils, and a rolling cart (shown here with food atop it) can be wheeled wherever auxiliary work space is needed.

Catering supplies are kept completely separate from those used for family cooking. A recent kitchen remodeling added a pantry outfitted to store restaurant-size containers of foodstuffs. Installed in the basement, several large refrigerators and freezers are used solely for the business.

The caterer takes orders from a kitchen command post equipped with a desk, telephone, and large calendar. For inspiration, she turns to cooking magazines filed in a rack behind the basement door.

Transporting food can be as formidable a task as preparing it. This caterer chauffeurs her meals from kitchen to airport in a Jeep Wagoneer that gets to the airport regardless of weather. She outfitted it by installing foam panels in back, then driving to a restaurant supply house, where she tried combinations of heavy-duty plastic containers until she found pieces that exactly fill the back of the vehicle. This arrangement keeps food from sliding around while she drives. Corrugated sheets of disposable plastic foam in the bottoms of the containers further secure serving plates. Camping-style coolers keep perishables from spoiling.

COOKING BY THE BOOKS

If you're considering home catering, familiarize yourself with local zoning and health code regulations before you test your first recipe. Some communities flat-out forbid using home kitchens to prepare food served to the public; others permit it, but you'll usually have to make specific changes to gain approval.

You may know someone who runs a home catering service without regard to regulations, but to do so involves considerable risks. In addition to possible governmental penalties, you may be liable for lawsuits from any customer who becomes ill from your food.

In many communities local authorities permit a limited amount of baking in ordinary home kitchens, such as providing cakes and cookies for charity sales. But usually if your sales exceed about $2,000 a year, you're considered a commercial operator.

Serving food to the public means ensuring that what they eat is free from contamination. You may be convinced that your home kitchen is clean, and know that no one has ever become sick from food you've prepared. Families, however, usually share resistance to household germs that outsiders might be vulnerable to. More important, perishable foods, such as those containing meat, fish, poultry, or milk products, can support the growth of disease-causing microorganisms unless kept properly refrigerated. Most ordinary home kitchens lack sufficient refrigerated storage to adequately protect the large quantities of food required for catering.

What sorts of changes will you need to make to have your kitchen comply with government standards? The federal government's Food and Drug Administration issues suggested guidelines for commercial kitchens; local regulations are as strict or stricter than these guidelines. Consult local authorities for their specifics; here are some general points to consider.

• The catering kitchen and all related food storage must be separate from the home kitchen. Many home caterers set up their professional kitchens in other areas, such as a basement or addition, which are licensed and inspected regularly.

Food containers must be stored a minimum of 6 inches above the floor, and the design of the storage area must facilitate easy cleaning.

• You must install a three-compartment sink for washing dishes: one basin for soapy water, one for clear rinse water, and the third for a chemical sanitizer. A commercial dishwasher with water temperatures of 180 to 200 degrees F can substitute.

• Refrigeration must be adequate to protect food that can spoil before and after it's prepared. This means, for example, being able to refrigerate a wedding's worth of hors d'oeuvres between the time they're made and the time they're served.

Use an accurate thermometer to monitor refrigerator temperatures, which should be at or below 45 degrees F; store frozen food at 0 degrees F or below.

• Animals, as well as people other than authorized workers, are forbidden in the kitchen. (This means no children and no pets.)

• The kinds of food you prepare determine many specific kitchen requirements. Baked goods, for example, don't support the growth of bacteria the way chicken salad does, and storage requirements would differ accordingly.

How you serve the food affects sanitation requirements, as well. The food pictured *opposite,* for example, is packaged in individual disposable containers, eliminating the reuse of dishes and utensils.

If you're just starting out and are not sure whether you want to invest in major home modifications, or in buying or signing a lease for a commercial kitchen, look for an already licensed commercial kitchen that you can use or rent part-time or seasonally. Kitchens in churches, fire stations, or restaurants that are not open year-round are all possibilities.

A GUESTHOUSE

Have your children grown and left you with a large house full of empty rooms? Is your home located in an especially scenic spot or near a popular tourist attraction? Do you yearn to leave the city, but wonder how you'll earn a living far from the urban job market? If your answer to any of these questions is yes, turning your home into a guesthouse or purchasing an inn might be a satisfying and profitable venture.

The two guest cottages pictured *above* are part of a 120-acre Wisconsin farm. The owners live on the property in a rambling house, six of whose bedrooms are reserved for guests. Derelict when purchased, the farm buildings have been painstakingly restored inside and out. (For views of the entire farm complex, see pages 20 and 21.)

The cottage in the center of the photo *above* was moved from a neighboring farm and installed atop concrete foundation pillars. When it first arrived, only three walls remained, and exposure to the elements had damaged the interior. A fourth wall, a new cedar shingle roof, siding, a porch, and an ironstone fascia around the foundation were added in what amounts to a nearly total rebuilding of the original dilapidated structure.

Inside as well as out
The owners also breathed new life into the interior shown *op-*

posite. Painted fir wainscoting provides a soft backdrop for a collection of country furnishings and accessories. A collection of old farm implements mounted on one wall reminds visitors of the cottage's former life as a tractor shed.

An extra-high bed platform leaves room for storage underneath. A delicately colored quilt and working wood stove keep guests cozy on winter nights.

The cottages do not have their own bathrooms; guests use modern facilities in a nearby renovated barn. The barn also houses a sauna and swimming pool.

Rules and regulations
If you're interested in becoming an innkeeper, you'll need to thoroughly research local zoning and licensing laws. Regulations vary, but, as a rule, private homes that offer ''bed and breakfast'' to no more than two guest families are neither licensed nor inspected by government agen-

cies. To fit into this unregulated category, the proprietors usually must adhere to certain guidelines. These may include the following:
• The guesthouse is also the family home of the host or hostess.
• The owners agree not to advertise; all publicity is by word of mouth.
• Only lodgers who've made reservations will be accepted as guests.
• Food can be served only to the overnight guests. The guesthouse may not also operate as a restaurant.

Guesthouses that provide accommodations to more than two families or accept transient lodgers are considered hotels or motels and must meet all applicable commercial standards and regulations.

AN ORCHID-GROWER'S GREENHOUSE

Orchids are delicate beauties. One night of below-freezing temperatures or a few hours of 100-plus-degree heat could wipe out a collection that took years to build and cultivate. The orchid collector whose greenhouse is pictured here travels to the jungles of Central and South America to seek out rare specimens. When he returns to his North American home, he protects his transplanted blooms in a solar-heated, partly underground structure that provides the stable temperatures and humidity levels crucial to their survival.

Cultivating orchids is strictly a not-for-profit avocation for this collector. We've included his greenhouse in this chapter, however, because of the sophistication of its design, developed to combat the orchid-grower's nightmare—sudden power failures. After sleepless nights tending kerosene heaters, this collector collaborated with an engineer friend to design a solar-heated, in-ground greenhouse that keeps heat fluctuation to a minimum, regardless of temperatures outside.

Their design sinks the 24x24-foot greenhouse below the frost line, where ground temperatures average 55 degrees year-round. The stability of the ground temperature acts as superinsulation that helps maintain even temperatures winter and summer.

Solar heat is stored in three 12-foot-long rock bins encased in cinder blocks and lined with 3 inches of rigid foam insulation. During the day, a fan at the end of each bin gently pulls warm air from the top of the greenhouse down over the rocks, heating them. At night in the colder months, this operation is reversed; cooler air drawn over the rocks is warmed by their stored heat. The fans operate constantly, circulating air as well as helping to heat the greenhouse.

The collector also installed an auxiliary gas-fired hot-water heating system that kicks on if winter temperatures fall too low.

During the summer, an evaporative cooler pumps in cool air, and a manually operable 3x5-foot window at the top of the greenhouse's north wall vents excess heat.

A SHEEP RANCH

Unhappy with her 9-to-5 office job as a graphic designer, this entrepreneur left the city and founded a cottage industry that produces handmade woolens—starting with the sheep. The "cottage" is actually an 80-acre farm that supports a flock of 60 black and white sheep. Neighbors knit the sweaters to her design specifications; her lawyer husband handles the financial side of the business and plans marketing strategies.

St. Marys Woolens began as a venture to raise sheep for meat and fleece for sale, but the lambs were saved from slaughter when the owner learned how to hand-spin wool. Success at spinning left her with plenty of yarn and a desire to put it to good use.

On a trip to a state fair, she met a dealer in knitting machines who offered free instruction along with the purchase of a machine. She took him up on the offer, brought the machine home, and tried her hand at sweater design. Her early creations quickly sold out at local Christmas bazaars, and from then on, business has boomed.

Meeting a growing demand

Today, sheep are raised and sheared on the farm; then the fleeces, shown *opposite,* are shipped to a mill that still uses nineteenth-century spinning machines. Yarn produced on the mill's old-fashioned "mule-spinners" looks and feels very much like handspun yarn.

In addition to pure black and white yarn, the mill combines various proportions of the two to produce several shades of gray. The wool is not dyed or chemically treated in any way, so it retains natural lanolin that helps it shed rain and snow. Cones of the spun wool are shown stacked on shelves along with finished garments in the photo *at upper right.*

Back at the farm, the owner works out new designs for the St. Marys line of sweaters, vests, mittens, scarves, and

leg warmers on her own knitting machine. She supplies farm neighbors with looms and teaches them how to use the looms. Following her patterns, each home knitter meets a quota of 10 sweaters a week. The owner then blocks and hand-seams the garments.

The couple sell the woolens on weekends from their own small shop in a local shopping mall. They also market their goods through larger stores in their home state, out-of-state boutiques, and mail order catalogs.

If you're considering a similar cottage operation where piecework will be subcontracted to home workers, consult your state labor department to find out what regulations govern this kind of employment in your area. More about this on pages 106 and 107.

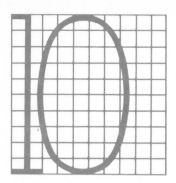

A PLACE FOR YOUR HOBBY

Even the most dedicated worker needs some time off from the job, and this final chapter will show you how to make room for your nonbusiness interests. The same planning that goes into creating a successful workplace can improve the places you spend your at-home leisure hours. Sewing, collecting model trains, appreciating the best that music and video have to offer, gardening, pursuing physical culture—whatever your hobby, having a special place for it will let you enjoy your leisure-time activity more, and more often.

Taking a cue from efficient kitchen design, this sewing room revolves around a laminate-covered island—a 3x3x7½-foot unit that provides ample work space for spreading fabric, laying out and cutting patterns, and piecing quilts. Grooves in the laminate top, pictured *below,* let the owner lay fabric across a groove, then cut easily in a straight line.

Four drawers at the end of the island organize thread, trim, and patterns. Dowels installed in the shallow top drawer hold spools upright. Below, two partitioned drawers store packages of braid and trim on their sides so colors are visible at a glance. The 10-inch-deep bottom drawer holds patterns vertically to simplify filing and finding.

A boxed fluorescent fixture mounted on the underside of the hanging cabinet illuminates the work surface. Natural light filters through a leaded-glass transom over doors to a hallway that boasts a 5x6-foot skylight.

At one end of the room, a second work station, pictured in the rear of the photo *opposite,* features a laminate-topped counter with storage cabinets below.

Rather than incorporate the sewing machine into either the island or the counter, the owner placed it on a separate table beneath a pair of windows. This location lets her enjoy a view to a deck outside while she sews. The sewing-machine table also divides the room into three distinct work stations, allowing several family members to comfortably share the sewing room, or one person to work on several projects at the same time.

MODEL TRAINS

A miniature locomotive chugging down its track is irresistible to just about any child—or former child—and the chief engineer of this line enjoys initiating his grandchildren into the fascinating world of model trains. Still under construction, this railroad will one day make its way through three-dimensional tunnels, over bridges and mountains, and past waterfalls. The overall plan evolved from a few rough sketches and lots of improvisation, fueled by the imagination of its creator.

The 12x35-foot train room pictured here began a decade ago as a single loop of track on the floor of the living room upstairs. Greatly expanded in size and complexity, it still bears its original name, "The Living Room Empire."

The Empire's creator collects Lionel 027-scale trains—the big, fun-to-play-with toy trains that he always wanted when he was a boy. Because these trains are collectors' items, he has kept all of the original boxes for the power units and hundreds of pieces of rolling stock; they're stacked beneath the hardboard surface on which the trains run. Shelves and tables, connected by a lumber framework, support the surface.

The train layout illustrated *below* includes switching yards, a passenger station, engine storage facilities, and a mainline track circling the entire basement.

The train room has become an extended family project, including scenic backgrounds painted with acrylics on gesso-primed hardboard sheets by the owner's son-in-law.

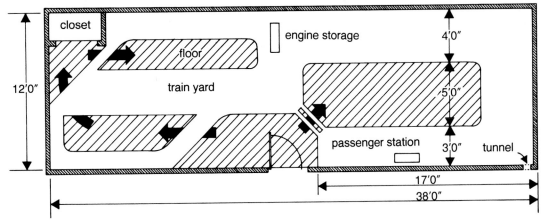

SOUND AND VIDEO ENTERTAINMENT

Nearly every American family owns at least one television set. Today, the options of watching what we want when we want, and of showing feature films at home, lead many of us to purchase videocassette player/recorders, as well. Add to these a stereo system for listening to radio, tapes, and records (and amplifying TV sound), a video game cartridge system, and perhaps a home computer that ties into the TV screen, and you're faced with a formidable collection of machines, wires, and cables. If you're bringing the electronic age home, you'll want to plan a place where you and your equipment can comfortably coexist.

No matter where it's located, a home entertainment center requires three essentials: good acoustics, a clear sight line to the TV screen, and comfortable, flexible furnishings.

Sound travels in waves from the source to your ears. Along the way, it's reflected and absorbed in varying degrees by the surfaces in the room. Hard surfaces, such as bare walls, floors, and ceilings, reflect sound; soft ones, such as carpeting, upholstered furniture, and curtains, absorb a portion of sound waves. A ratio of about three-fourths hard to one-fourth soft surfaces is ideal for listening, and most family rooms or living rooms approximate these proportions. If the sound in a particular room seems either too dead and muffled or too harsh and ringing, experiment with the furniture arrangement, or add or subtract a few items, such as draperies and area rugs, to balance the sound.

To ensure that everyone has a good seat for viewing, plan to be able to easily adjust either the TV set, the seating, or both. Mounting the TV set on a pullout turntable or placing it on a rolling stand gives you control. Swivel chairs, modular seating pieces, or large floor cushions let viewers position themselves comfortably.

Getting the big picture
If you opt for a large-screen TV, you'll need to work the projection unit and screen into your logistics. Two-piece systems (a separate projector and screen) often incorporate the projector into a coffee-table unit. With this type of system, nothing must block the path between projector and screen. To circumvent this limitation, some units feature projectors that mount on the ceiling.

With two-piece units, the greater the distance from the projector to the screen, the larger the image. For small rooms, where you may not have adequate distance between the projector and the screen, a one-piece system can offer a solution. The projector and screen fold out of a single piece of furniture that extends from the wall three to four feet when open. A mirror reflects the projected image onto the screen.

For any type of TV viewing, you'll want to avoid light that shines onto the screen or into viewers' eyes. Lighting controlled by a dimmer switch and installed behind the seating area and well above or below eye level keeps glare, both direct and reflected, out of the picture.

Housing the components
Massing your equipment on one wall gives a neat, organized look to a room, simplifies hookups, and conceals the maze of wires. The best arrangement lets you easily gain access to the backs of the units without moving them. Shelves or custom cabinets with open or removable backs work well. Electronic equipment is sensitive to heat and moisture, so be sure to leave space around each piece of equipment for ventilation.

In the combination family room and guest bedroom pictured *at left,* stereo speakers and video components are combined in a compact, custom-built cabinet hung from the wall beneath a large window. Carpeted platforms, topped with large, black cushions, offer comfortable seating for the entire family. A platform bed in the foreground, which projects diagonally from a corner, serves for guest sleeping.

A PLACE FOR YOUR HOBBY

GREENHOUSE GARDENING

If your love of gardening extends beyond a few potted plants on the windowsill, consider letting your hobby take root in a greenhouse. Bumping-out a kitchen window with a cantilevered prefab glass unit requires no foundation work. Screw the unit into a wooden frame built around the window, install shelves for pots, and turn your green thumb loose. For more ambitious gardening, consider a larger prefab unit with foundation and flooring, or a custom-built structure with space for a whole crop of containerized vegetables or an abundance of foliage and flowers.

Fast and healthy food makes a quick trip from plant to plate, thanks to the food-producing greenhouse adjoining the kitchen pictured *at right*. Here, a variety of containerized vegetables and herbs flourish year-round.

This greenhouse was designed to fit unobtrusively under the roofline of a U-shape ranch house. Glazed sections in the roof let winter sun stream in. In summer, adjustable shades modulate light and heat to protect plants from too-strong midday sun.

Doors open from the kitchen to the greenhouse and from the greenhouse to the backyard. In winter, the owners open the kitchen door to allow solar heat from the greenhouse to flow into the main living space. In summer, opening the door to the outside brings in fresh air and helps keep the greenhouse from overheating. If temperatures in the greenhouse rise too high, a thermostatically controlled fan goes on automatically

It takes more than a watering can to efficiently quench the thirst of a garden of this size. A convenient spigot and hose simplify watering. Ceramic tile over a concrete slab floor takes spills and soil in stride. A drain in the center of the floor handles runoff and allows the owners to hose down the entire space when necessary.

The walls and ceiling are lined with hardy, moisture-resistant redwood. Sturdy built-in shelves supplement floor space and ensure that all plants have access to the sun.

When tomatoes, pole beans, and peas get tall, the owners string wire or twine from the ceiling beams to support the plants. When this photograph was taken, these vegetables had just been harvested and removed. Pictured here are new young plants—including chives, lettuce, cabbage, artichokes, peppers, and broccoli—which will be transplanted into larger containers as they outgrow the old ones. On the greenhouse floor, a potted kumquat tree bears fruit.

Prefabricated alternatives
The configuration of this home easily incorporates a greenhouse. In a more conventional home, a lean-to style greenhouse could be attached to an exterior wall, with a door to connect the greenhouse with living space. Because the greenhouse shares a wall with the main house, you can tap into existing heating, electrical, and plumbing systems.

The most popular prefab lean-to units feature sturdy aluminum frames and glass walls. Less expensive, but also less durable, are wood-frame units covered with plastic film.

In cold climates, gardeners usually favor structures with a low wall of stone, brick, or wood at ground level, and glass above that. The wall helps the greenhouse retain heat in winter. Units with glass extending all the way to the ground are practical choices in milder regions. All-glass construction maximizes usable growing space.

If possible, try to locate your greenhouse facing south; this orientation will let in as much winter sun as possible. Next in order of preference come southeast, southwest, and west exposures. A north-facing greenhouse will accommodate only hardy foliage plants.

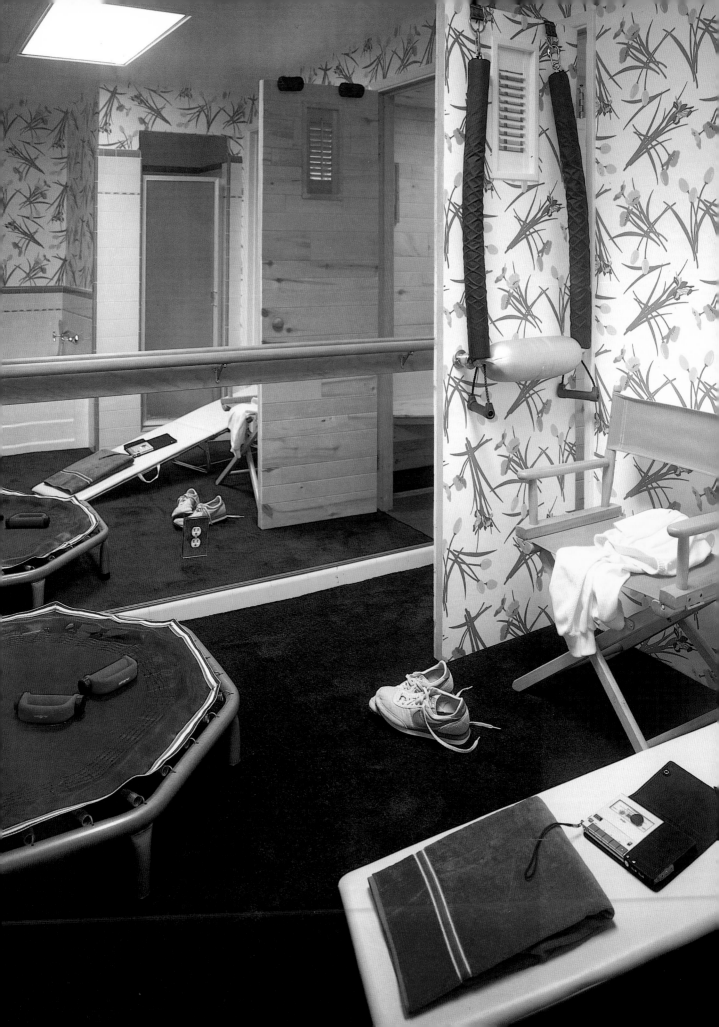

A PLACE FOR YOUR HOBBY

HOME EXERCISE

We all know that daily exercise is good for us, yet many of us are equally good at putting it off until tomorrow. In the midst of a hectic schedule, it can be hard to squeeze in a trip to the gym, health club, or dance studio. An at-home exercise center lets you work out without having to go out, and that means that even short blocks of time can become productive fitness sessions. If you're a confirmed fitness buff, visits to the exercise center can be the high point of your day. And if you're just starting out on a shape-up program, what better inspiration than a room filled with efficient-looking equipment ready for use?

This well-appointed exercise center started life as a white-elephant bathroom in an older home. With a badly cracked tile floor and a damaged ceiling, its greatest asset was its size. The homeowners, both sports enthusiasts, decided that the 11x15-foot space was large enough to accommodate their exercise equipment and a sauna, along with complete bathroom facilities.

If you don't have an oversize bathroom, scout other suitable locations to set up an exercise center. For those who enjoy starting the day with exercises, a center in or off the master bedroom is especially convenient and private. A center in the family room works well if fitness is a shared family activity.

In this home, the original bathroom fixtures and the 1940s yellow-and-aqua tile surrounding the tub and shower stall were in good condition, so the owners retained the tile and selected a floral wall covering that picks up the tile colors. A sink that used to hang on the wall where the director's chair is now was moved into the toilet area behind closed doors.

Special extras

An adjacent linen closet was converted to a sauna for two. You can have a sauna designed to fit a particular space or build one from a kit in dimensions ranging from 28x42x78 inches to 8x10x7 feet. A simple closet conversion can be accomplished by purchasing a "door kit." Built into the door is all the necessary equipment to produce the sauna's dry heat. To install one, replace the original door with the kit door, insulate the closet, and add a bench about 2 feet wide to relax on. Use well-seasoned wood free of knots for the bench. Inset or cover any nails to prevent burns. Sauna aficionados follow 10 to 30 minutes in the sauna with a cool shower, so try to locate your sauna near one.

Mirroring the wall opposite the tub visually expands the compact quarters, and provides a view for checking correct positions for dance and exercise. The ballet bar was recycled from an old stair railing.

The skylight is really an impostor, made by cutting an opening in the dropped ceiling, and hiding recessed fluorescent tubes behind a white acrylic lens.

To create a level, resilient floor, the owners filled in depressions in the broken tile floor, and installed thick padding topped with low-pile plush carpeting.

A mini trampoline provides a chance for an indoor aerobic workout when bad weather precludes jogging. A "G-swing" used for inversion exercises hangs over the sauna door, and a slant board facilitates a variety of toning and strengthening exercises. To free the entire area for floor exercises, the board and trampoline stow against a wall, or in the sauna when it's not in use. The box at left gives dimensions of standard exercise equipment. To learn more about planning an exercise center for your home, turn the page.

NUMBERS TO KNOW

- Floor-mounted weight lifting machine: 96" wide x 96" long x 84" high (includes clearance for using it)
- Wall-mounted weight lifting machine: 82" wide x 96" long x 84" high (includes clearance for using it)
- Weight bench: 5'4" long x 14" wide, knee-post 38" high
- Treadmill: 6'6" long x 22" wide
- Exercise bicycle: 38" long (seat adjusts from 22" to 40")
- Exercise mats: 2'x6' to 5'x10'
- Rowing machine: 2'x4' (plus elbowroom on each side)
- Small trampoline (rebounder): 3½' diameter
- Slant board: 6' long

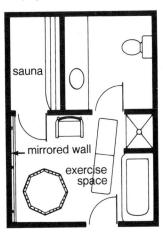

sauna

mirrored wall

exercise space

This basement workout center had a concrete floor, a poor surface for exercising. To improve it, the owners built a raised wooden platform and topped it with impact-absorbing tile.

PLANNING A HOME EXERCISE CENTER

The shower at left provides facilities for freshening up after workouts. At right, laundry equipment allows for cleanup of exercise clothes and towels, so they need never leave the area.

A home exercise center can be as basic as a mat you unroll on the floor, or as complete as a gym, with a variety of equipment, free weights, and even amenities for after-workout relaxing, such as a shower, sauna, or whirlpool. How large a space you need depends on your fitness program and the activities and equipment it requires.

If your program includes free weights, make sure your storage facility can handle the load. In our drawing, a wall was strengthened to hold a full set of weights on slanted shelves.

If space permits, try to arrange your center so that most of the equipment can stay in place full time. Lugging equipment in and out of closets provides exercise, but the kind that's likely to discourage you from making the best use of the facility.

The center illustrated here is set up in a basement, a location that's convenient in many homes. You'll usually have enough room to spread out, and if your laundry is down below, too, soiled workout clothes can go directly into the washer and dryer. To streamline even more, plan closets, cabinets, or other storage to accommodate towels and exercise clothing.

To prevent injuries, you'll want a floor that can absorb and cushion the impact of activities such as jogging, skipping rope, and aerobics. If the present floor is concrete, consider making changes to increase its resiliency. One solution is to build a wooden framework and install a plywood platform over the concrete. Top the plywood floor with a thick rubberized mat. Another way to add resiliency, without a platform, is to purchase ½-inch-thick interlocking rubber tiles designed for exercise facilities.

Make sure your space has adequate ventilation. Operable windows or a door that opens to the outside are ideal, but if your center is in a basement that lacks them, install a fan or two to move air.

A full-length mirror lets you correct posture, practice dance or martial arts, and receive instant feedback on body-building and weight loss.

Lighting should be cheerful, but not glaring. You'll be lying on your back to perform many exercises, so be sure that unshielded lights will not shine directly into your eyes.

Music can enliven your routine, so plan to keep a radio, cassette player, or stereo in your center. Exercise tapes and records also can offer welcome variety. If you like to exercise along with a TV instructor, you also may want to include a TV set or videocassette player.

CRAFTING WREATHS AND MAKING TEDDY BEARS

If you don't have a spare room to devote to your hobby, you can still create a well-outfitted area that's far more efficient than a kitchen table commandeered between meals. The trick is to stake out a territory with sufficient space to store your supplies and tools and a work surface where you can spread out materials. Ideally, you'll want a place sufficiently separated from other family activities so that works in progress won't be in the way. Two mother-and-daughter pairs set up the hobby centers pictured here: one in a hallway, the other in a corner of a family room.

Examine the photo *below* to see how a wall-hugging counter, combined with customized storage, turned a hallway leading to a furnace room into a workplace for crafting wreaths. Beneath the 18-inch-deep laminate counter, stacking plastic storage bins hold supplies. A chest at one end of the hallway and a deep shelf above it store bulky materials. Mounted between two wooden brackets, a ½-inch dowel holds ribbons so that they can be unwound as needed and cut without tangling. A shallow shelf above the dowel holds tins of small ornaments.

Wreath forms made of straw, grapevines, and twigs hang from 1-inch dowels at far left. A wire running the length of the room suspends clumps of grasses, dried eucalyptus, and wheat stalks used to complete the wreaths.

Bear necessities

The miniature teddy bear factory pictured *opposite* tucks into a cozy corner next to a fireplace. Closed cupboards hide bulky bags of polyester stuffing for the bear innards, jars and boxes of joints, eyes, noses, and trim, and patterns for a dozen different sizes of bears. Each pattern is color-keyed and placed in a separate manila envelope for easy retrieval.

Open shelves display assorted members of a large bear collection, along with folded fabric already cut to the dimensions of the different patterns.

A sewing machine occupies one end of the table, just out of camera range. Baskets corral pins, needles, spools of thread, and other implements.

The bear-makers often give lessons, and several crafters can comfortably work at the table. Each student machine-stitches the pieces at home, then returns with finished pieces ready to be assembled.

WHERE TO GO FOR MORE INFORMATION

Better Homes and Gardens® Books
Want to learn more about finding and setting up home work space? These Better Homes and Gardens® books can help.

Better Homes and Gardens®
NEW DECORATING BOOK
How to translate ideas into workable solutions for every room in your home. Choosing a style, furniture arrangements, windows, walls and ceilings, floors, lighting, and accessories. 433 color photos, 76 how-to illustrations, 432 pages.

Better Homes and Gardens®
DOLLAR-STRETCHING DECORATING
An excellent source for ideas and projects that make your dollar work harder. Shows how to use imagination, ingenuity, and know-how to sidestep high costs while stepping up in style, comfort, and quality. Filled with easy-to-accomplish ideas, practical suggestions, do-it-yourself projects, and how-to drawings. 192 pages.

Better Homes and Gardens®
COMPLETE GUIDE TO HOME REPAIR,
MAINTENANCE, & IMPROVEMENT
Inside your home, outside your home, your home's systems, basics you should know. Anatomy and step-by-step drawings illustrate components, tools, techniques, and finishes.
515 how-to techniques; 75 charts; 2,734 illustrations; 552 pages.

Better Homes and Gardens®
STEP-BY-STEP BUILDING SERIES
A series of do-it-yourself building books that provides step-by-step illustrations and how-to information for starting and finishing many common construction projects and repair jobs around your house. More than 90 projects and 1,200 illustrations in this series of six 96-page books:
STEP-BY-STEP BASIC PLUMBING
STEP-BY-STEP BASIC WIRING
STEP-BY-STEP BASIC CARPENTRY
STEP-BY-STEP HOUSEHOLD REPAIRS
STEP-BY-STEP MASONRY & CONCRETE
STEP-BY-STEP CABINETS & SHELVES

Other Sources of Information
The government is a major source of information about setting up your own business, whether home-based or not. For more information, write to:

Small Business Administration. Consult your local telephone directory for the SBA office closest to you.

Other helpful sources include a variety of books and publications. The following are just a few that you may find useful.

Small Business Reporter
A series of publications available at a nominal cost from:
Bank of America
Dept. 3401
P.O. Box 37000
San Francisco, CA 94137

The Office Book: Ideas and Designs for Contemporary Work Spaces, by Judy Graf Klein. New York: Facts on File, 1982.

Women Working Home: The Homebased Business Guide and Directory, by Marion Behr and Wendy Lazar. Edison, NJ: WWH Press, 1981.

Workstead: Living and Working in the Same Place, by Jeremy Joan Hewes. New York: Doubleday, 1981.

ACKNOWLEDGMENTS

Architects and Designers

The following is a page-by-page listing of the architects and designers whose work appears in this book.

Pages 8-9
  Jim McQuiston, Archonics
Page 11
  Agnes C. Bourne, ASID
Pages 12-13
  Sterling Kenty
Pages 16-17
  Woody Gruber
Pages 18-19
  Marty Halverson
Pages 20-21
  Suzanne Moore-Wollum
Pages 34-35
  Rita Hooker
Page 36
  Peter Rodi, Designbank
Page 37
  Lynne and Terry Scott
Pages 38-39
  Carl Strona, AIA
Pages 40-41
  Donna Warner
Page 42
  School of Family Resources and Consumer Sciences, University of Wisconsin, Madison
Pages 46-47
  George A. Barker, AIA Principal Architects Mosher, Drew, Watson, and Ferguson
Pages 48-49
  Ted Smith, AIA
Pages 50-51
  Borrelli & Associates
Page 52
  Don Roberts/Roberts Associates. Architects, Planners

Page 53
  John Bruton and Michele Olson
Pages 56-57
  Michael Borrelli and Bob Dean
Pages 60-61
  Saati Associates
Pages 62-63
  Michael Goard
Pages 64-65
  Carol Bruns
Pages 66-69
  John Davis and Joan Rosen
Pages 70-72
  Shirley A. Held
Pages 74-75
  Peter Powell, Mark Beck Associates
Pages 76-77
  Michael J. Plautz
Pages 78-79
  Woody Gruber
Pages 84-85
  Peter Sussman
Pages 86-87
  George Skluzacek
Pages 110-111
  Sharon Schnackenberg
Pages 112-113
  Daniel Feidt
Pages 116-117
  Robert Adler, DDS
Pages 114-115
  Richard C. Shepard
Pages 120-121
  Ferris Cordner, Thomas Design Inc.
Pages 122-123
  James A. Hufnagel
Pages 124-125
  Vaike Radamus, ASID
Pages 130-131
  Elaine Froehlich
Pages 132-133
  Patty McDonald
Pages 138-139
  Bob Benson

Pages 128-129
  McNerney & Carrow
Pages 134-135
  Linda Joan Smith
Pages 136-137
  Suzanne Moore-Wollum
Pages 140-141
  Cathy Mountain, St. Mary's Woolens
Pages 142-143
  Harry A. Jacobs, AIA
Pages 144-145
  Robert Hermann
Pages 146-147
  Sam and Lynn Rosenberg
Pages 148-149
  Ron Gondek
Pages 150-151
  Judy Ferguson and Joan Gillespie
Page 154
  Joan Bekins
Page 155
  Donna Martin

Photographers and Illustrators

We extend our thanks to the following photographers and illustrators whose creative talents and technical skills contributed much to this book.

Charles Ashley
Ernest Braun
Ross Chapple
Mike Dieter
Steven Fridge
Hedrich-Blessing
Hopkins Associates
William N. Hopkins
Peter Lewitt
Scott Little
Fred Lyon
Maris/Semel
Bradley Olman
Jessie Walker

INDEX

Page numbers in *italics* refer to photographs or illustrations.